# THE SMALL BUSINESS OWNER'S TAX GUIDE

*A Practical Guide to Smart Taxes for Entrepreneurs and Small Business Owners*



*By*

**BRANDON K. MOORE**

**Copyright & Disclaimer**



Printed in the United States of America.
ISBN (tbd)

# Acknowledgments

To every entrepreneur who decided to take the leap and build something from nothing—this guide is for you. Thank you to my clients, colleagues, and fellow small business owners who've trusted me over the years with your questions, your stories, and your financial goals. You inspire this work every day.

# Preface

Owning a small business is one of the most rewarding—and challenging—journeys you can take. Taxes are part of that story, and while they may not be glamorous, they are one of the most powerful tools for protecting your profits and fueling your future growth.

I wrote this guide to help entrepreneurs like you understand not only *what* to do, but *why* it matters. Whether you're launching your first LLC, hiring your first employee, or preparing for your best year yet, you'll find clear explanations, actionable steps, and professional insights designed for real business life.

Let's simplify taxes, reduce the stress, and keep more of what you earn.

— **Brandon K. Moore**

# Table of Contents

*Chapter 1*

# Why Taxes Matter More Than You Think

When you first start a business, taxes usually sit somewhere near the bottom of your excitement list—somewhere between "renew business license" and "figure out payroll software." Yet taxes shape every part of your business story: your cash flow, your pricing, your investment decisions, even your mindset as an owner.

## THE TAX MINDSET

The most successful business owners I've worked with share one trait: they view taxes not as punishment, but as part of their financial strategy. Taxes are the single largest expense for most entrepreneurs—often more than rent, supplies, or payroll combined. Learning to manage them wisely is the difference between constant cash-flow anxiety and long-term stability.

> **Pro Tip:** *Treat taxes like any other bill you plan for. When you budget monthly for marketing, payroll, or insurance, set aside a percentage for taxes—typically 20–30% of profits depending on your structure.*

## HOW TAXES REFLECT YOUR BUSINESS STORY

Your tax return tells a story about your business—its growth, its margins, and how you steward your resources. A messy tax return often mirrors a messy business. Clean records, accurate deductions, and timely filing reflect professionalism and build credibility with lenders, partners, and clients.

**Example:**

| Scenario | Net Profit | Estimated Tax Rate | Taxes Owed |
|---|---|---|---|
| Unplanned | $100,000 | 30% | $30,000 |
| Planned (quarterly savings set aside 25%) | $100,000 | 30% | $30,000 → $25,000 saved |

Planning ahead turns a year-end panic into a smooth close-out.

## THE COST OF IGNORING TAXES

Ignoring your tax responsibilities is more expensive than paying them on time. Late penalties, interest, and the stress of back-tax notices add up quickly.

**Avoid This Mistake:** Waiting until April to "see what happens." Successful owners review financials monthly and meet with their CPA quarterly. Procrastination costs thousands.

## STEWARDSHIP, NOT JUST COMPLIANCE

Managing taxes isn't only about staying out of trouble—it's about stewardship. You're responsible for the financial health of your enterprise, your employees, and your own household. A well-planned tax strategy is a form of integrity: doing the right thing with the resources entrusted to you.

## YOUR NEXT STEP

*Quick Checklist:*

- ☑ Set up a separate business checking account
- ☑ Track income and expenses from day one
- ☑ Schedule a quarterly tax review
- ☑ Choose bookkeeping software or a CPA firm
- ☑ Create a "tax savings" sub-account and fund it monthly

**Pro Tip:** *Make your tax habits automatic—link your business account to a high-yield savings account and auto-transfer a fixed percentage of revenue each month.*

*Chapter 2*

# Choosing the Right Business Entity

*How the Structure You Choose Shapes Your Taxes, Liability, and Growth*

When you launch a business, few decisions carry more long-term impact than how you choose to structure it. Your **business entity** determines how you pay taxes, how you take money out, how you protect yourself legally, and even how investors view you.

Too many entrepreneurs skip this step or simply "check a box" on a form without understanding what it means. Let's fix that.

## UNDERSTANDING THE BASICS

At the core, your entity type affects two major areas:

- **Liability protection** — how much personal risk you carry.
- **Taxation** — how your profits are reported and taxed.

Here are the most common structures for small business owners:

| Entity Type | Liability Protection | Taxation Method | Ideal For |
|---|---|---|---|
| **Sole Proprietorship** | None | Individual tax return (Schedule C) | Freelancers, side hustles, low-risk startups |
| **Limited Liability Company (LLC)** | Moderate (depends on state) | Default: Pass-through (Schedule C or K-1) | Solo owners or small partnerships |

| Entity Type | Liability Protection | Taxation Method | Ideal For |
|---|---|---|---|
| **S Corporation (S-Corp)** | Strong | Pass-through with self-employment tax savings | Growing small businesses, service professionals |
| **C Corporation (C-Corp)** | Strong | Separate corporate tax return | Startups seeking investment, multiple shareholders |

## SOLE PROPRIETORSHIP: THE SIMPLEST START

A **sole proprietorship** is the easiest form—just you, your business income, and a Schedule C on your personal return.

It requires no formal filing beyond your local business license, but it also offers no liability protection. If the business is sued or incurs debt, your personal assets are at risk.

> **Pro Tip:** *If you're testing a new idea or freelancing, start as a sole proprietor—but once your revenue grows beyond $30,000–$50,000 or you sign contracts with clients, it's time to form an LLC.*

**Avoid This Mistake:** Mixing personal and business finances. Even as a sole proprietor, open a dedicated bank account and use it exclusively for business transactions.

## LIMITED LIABILITY COMPANY (LLC): THE MODERN DEFAULT

An **LLC** (Limited Liability Company) offers the best of both worlds for most small business owners. It's simple to form, provides liability protection, and offers flexible taxation options.

### How Taxes Work for LLCs

By default, a single-member LLC is taxed like a sole proprietorship, and a multi-member LLC is taxed like a partnership.

However, you can **elect to be taxed as an S-Corp** if your profits justify it—allowing you to save on self-employment taxes (we'll explore this in detail shortly).

**Example:**

If your LLC earns $100,000 net income:

- As a sole proprietorship, all $100,000 is subject to self-employment tax.
- As an S-Corp election, you might pay yourself a $60,000 salary and take $40,000 as a distribution—reducing self-employment tax on the latter portion.

*Quick Checklist: Setting Up an LLC*

- ☑ Check your state's Secretary of State website for availability
- ☑ File Articles of Organization
- ☑ Create an Operating Agreement
- ☑ Obtain an EIN from the IRS
- ☑ Open a business bank account
- ☑ Apply for any required local licenses

**Pro Tip:** *Keep your LLC's corporate veil intact—sign contracts under your business name, keep clean books, and don't pay personal bills from business accounts.*

## S CORPORATION: THE TAX SAVER

An **S Corporation** isn't a separate entity like an LLC or C-Corp—it's a **tax election** made with the IRS (Form 2553). But for many profitable small businesses, it's a smart move.

### Why It Matters

As an S-Corp, your business profits "pass through" to your personal tax return—just like an LLC—but you only pay **self-employment tax** on your *salary*, not on your total profit.

This structure can save thousands in taxes each year once your business consistently earns more than $40,000–$60,000 in net profit.

**Example:**

If you earn $100,000 in profit:

- As an LLC: pay self-employment tax on all $100,000
- As an S-Corp: pay yourself a $60,000 salary (subject to payroll taxes) and take $40,000 as a distribution (no self-employment tax)

**Pro Tip:** *The IRS expects your S-Corp salary to be "reasonable" for your role and industry. If you underpay yourself, you risk penalties. A CPA can benchmark this for you.*

**Avoid This Mistake:** Failing to run payroll. Even if you're the only owner, you must process W-2 payroll through your S-Corp, with proper withholdings and filings.

## C CORPORATION: THE GROWTH VEHICLE

A **C Corporation** is a separate legal and tax-paying entity. While less common for small local businesses, it's ideal for high-growth ventures or those seeking investors.

C-Corps pay their own corporate tax (currently 21% federal rate), and owners pay taxes again on dividends—known as **double taxation**. However, they can offer fringe benefits, stock options, and reinvest profits strategically.

*Quick Checklist: When a C-Corp Makes Sense*

- ☑ You plan to raise capital or add multiple shareholders
- ☑ You want to reinvest most profits instead of distributing them
- ☑ You offer employee stock or advanced benefits
- ☑ You anticipate an eventual sale or acquisition

**Pro Tip:** *Under Section 1202, Qualified Small Business Stock (QSBS) can exclude up to $10 million in capital gains for eligible C-Corp stock held more than five years—an advanced but powerful tax incentive.*

## CHOOSING THE RIGHT PATH

When deciding your structure, consider these three questions:

1. How much **risk** does your business carry?

2. How much **profit** do you expect to earn annually?
3. How much **complexity** are you willing to manage?

| Priority | Best Fit | Why |
|---|---|---|
| Simplicity | Sole Proprietor | Easiest setup, minimal paperwork |
| Flexibility | LLC | Protects assets, scalable, can elect S-Corp |
| Tax Efficiency | S-Corp | Reduces self-employment tax |
| Investment Potential | C-Corp | Access to funding and growth options |

## YOUR NEXT STEP

*Quick Checklist: Entity Decision Plan*

- ☑ Estimate your annual profit range
- ☑ Review liability risks (contracts, employees, assets)
- ☑ Discuss S-Corp election timing with your CPA
- ☑ File required state and IRS documents
- ☑ Update business licenses and bank accounts under the correct name

**Pro Tip:** *Revisit your entity choice every 1–2 years. As your business evolves, your structure should too.*

Next up:
**Chapter 3 – Recordkeeping Made Simple**
→ How to keep clean books, organize receipts, and simplify tax season without drowning in paperwork.

*Chapter 3*

# Recordkeeping Made Simple

*How Organized Books Can Save You Time, Money, and Stress*

For many small business owners, bookkeeping feels like the least glamorous part of entrepreneurship. But here's the truth: clean, organized financial records are one of your greatest competitive advantages. They save you money on taxes, help you make better decisions, and give you peace of mind when tax season arrives.

Good recordkeeping is not about perfection—it's about consistency.

## WHY IT MATTERS

Your business records form the foundation for:

- Accurate tax returns
- Smart business decisions
- Easier access to loans or lines of credit
- Better budgeting and cash flow management

When you know your numbers, you can lead your business confidently. When you don't, you're flying blind.

**Pro Tip:** *Think of your financial system like your car's dashboard. It doesn't make the engine run, but it tells you what's really happening under the hood.*

## THE CORE SYSTEM: INCOME, EXPENSES, ASSETS, AND LIABILITIES

Every business needs to track four basic categories:

| Category | What to Track | Example Tools |
|---|---|---|
| **Income** | All business revenue, sales, invoices | QuickBooks, Wave, Xero |
| **Expenses** | All deductible business costs | Expense tracking app, digital receipts |
| **Assets** | Equipment, property, and investments | Fixed asset schedule |
| **Liabilities** | Loans, credit cards, taxes payable | Balance sheet or accounting software |

When each of these is recorded properly, your financials tell a complete story. Miss one, and your taxes (and profits) start to blur.

## THE 3-ACCOUNT SYSTEM

To simplify your bookkeeping, create **three business accounts**:

1. **Operating Account** – for daily business income and expenses.
2. **Savings Account** – for taxes and emergency reserves.
3. **Owner's Pay Account** – for your personal transfers or distributions.

**Avoid This Mistake:** Running everything through one checking account. It creates confusion, invites IRS scrutiny, and makes cash flow impossible to manage.

**Pro Tip:** *Automate transfers each month—e.g., 20% of revenue to tax savings, 10% to reserves, and the rest to operating expenses.*

## TRACKING INCOME THE RIGHT WAY

Every dollar that flows into your business must be recorded. Whether you get paid by check, PayPal, or card, keep detailed records of:

- Client name
- Invoice number

- Payment method and date
- Description of service or product

**Example:**

If you earn $75,000 from 30 clients this year, a clean income log lets you quickly generate reports by month or client—helpful for both taxes and growth strategy.

*Quick Checklist: Income Tracking*

- ☑ Send professional invoices with sequential numbers
- ☑ Deposit payments into your business account (no cash co-mingling)
- ☑ Record payments in accounting software
- ☑ Match deposits to invoices monthly
- ☑ Keep digital copies of all invoices and receipts

## MANAGING EXPENSES WITHOUT THE CHAOS

Expense tracking is where most small business owners fall behind. The IRS allows deductions only for expenses that are **ordinary and necessary**—but you must be able to *prove* them.

**Pro Tip:** *Keep every receipt for $75 or more and digital copies for all recurring costs. Cloud-based accounting apps make this effortless—just snap a photo and upload.*

**Expense Categories to Track**

- Advertising and marketing
- Office supplies and software
- Rent or home office
- Business meals (50% deductible)
- Travel (airfare, hotels, mileage)
- Insurance premiums
- Professional fees (CPA, attorney, consultants)
- Education and training
- Equipment and depreciation

**Avoid This Mistake:** Using your personal credit card for business purchases. Mixing accounts can cause you to miss deductions and blur liability lines.

## RECEIPTS, RECORDS, AND RETENTION

How long should you keep records?

The IRS generally recommends **three years**, but some situations (like depreciable assets or unreported income) require up to **seven years**.

*Quick Checklist: Record Retention*

| Record Type | Keep For | Notes |
|---|---|---|
| Tax Returns | 7 years | Keep digital and printed copies |
| Receipts | 3–7 years | Keep digital backups |
| Payroll Records | 4 years | Required for employee taxes |
| Bank Statements | 3 years | Download PDFs annually |
| Loan Documents | Life of loan + 7 years | Especially for SBA loans |

**Pro Tip:** *Use cloud storage (e.g., Google Drive, Dropbox, or OneDrive) with folders for each year. Back up to an external hard drive once annually.*

## CHOOSING THE RIGHT SOFTWARE

Modern bookkeeping tools can automate 80% of your recordkeeping. Here are a few worth considering:

| Software | Best For | Features |
|---|---|---|
| **QuickBooks Online** | Most small businesses | Bank sync, invoicing, payroll |
| **Wave Accounting** | Freelancers & solopreneurs | Free, simple reporting |
| **Xero** | International or growing firms | Integrations, team access |
| **FreshBooks** | Service providers | Project-based billing |

**Pro Tip:** *Your time is valuable—if bookkeeping takes you more than two hours per week, it's time to hire help or outsource.*

## MONTHLY HABITS THAT KEEP YOU ON TRACK

*Quick Checklist: Monthly Bookkeeping Routine*

- ☑ Reconcile your bank and credit card accounts
- ☑ Review profit & loss (P&L) statement
- ☑ Categorize all new expenses
- ☑ Set aside tax savings based on profit
- ☑ Review outstanding invoices or bills
- ☑ Backup your accounting file

**Avoid This Mistake:** Waiting until tax season to "catch up." It doubles your stress and increases the chance of errors.

## WHEN TO HIRE A BOOKKEEPER OR CPA

If your business earns more than $100,000 per year or handles multiple accounts, hiring a professional bookkeeper is usually worth it. A CPA or tax advisor can:

- Review your books quarterly
- Spot tax-saving opportunities early
- Ensure compliance and audit readiness

**Pro Tip:** *Think of a bookkeeper as your "financial assistant" and your CPA as your "financial strategist." Both roles save you far more than they cost.*

## BRINGING IT ALL TOGETHER

Strong recordkeeping isn't about being an accountant—it's about taking ownership. Organized financials give you clarity, confidence, and control. When your books are clean, you make smarter decisions and sleep better at night.

*Quick Recap Checklist:*

- ☑ Separate all business accounts
- ☑ Track income and expenses digitally
- ☑ Back up all records monthly
- ☑ Reconcile accounts and review reports
- ☑ Schedule quarterly CPA check-ins

**Pro Tip:** *Consistency beats perfection. A small system you use every week will outperform a complex system you abandon after a month.*

Next up:
**Chapter 4 – What You Can (and Can't) Deduct**
→ A friendly guide to understanding legitimate business deductions, red flags to avoid, and how to confidently claim every dollar you deserve.

*Chapter 4*

# What You Can (and Can't) Deduct

*Understanding Legitimate Business Deductions and How to Claim Them Confidently*

The heart of smart tax strategy is simple: **document everything you spend for business** and **know what's deductible.**

Every dollar you can legitimately deduct lowers your taxable income, saving you real money.

Unfortunately, many small business owners leave thousands of dollars on the table each year simply because they don't know what qualifies—or they fear triggering an audit. This chapter will make it clear, practical, and stress-free.

## THE GOLDEN RULE OF DEDUCTIONS

According to the IRS, an expense must be both **"ordinary and necessary"** to be deductible.

- **Ordinary** means common in your trade or profession.
- **Necessary** means helpful and appropriate for your business.

> **Pro Tip:** *If you can clearly explain how an expense supports your business, it's probably deductible. If you hesitate or need to stretch the logic, it's probably not.*

## THE POWER OF SMALL DEDUCTIONS

Most business owners focus on big expenses—equipment, rent, or travel—but small recurring costs add up to major savings.

**Example:**

If you spend just $150 a month on software subscriptions, that's **$1,800 per year.**
At a 25% tax rate, that's **$450** in tax savings—just for tracking those small items.

## THE BIG FOUR DEDUCTION CATEGORIES

Let's start with the most common deductions every small business should review:

| Category | Examples | Notes |
|---|---|---|
| **Operational Expenses** | Office supplies, utilities, postage, repairs | Must be business-related, not personal use |
| **Administrative Costs** | Accounting, legal, payroll, professional fees | 100% deductible |
| **Marketing & Promotion** | Advertising, business cards, website hosting, social media ads | Includes creative design & consulting costs |
| **Employee & Contractor Pay** | Wages, benefits, contract labor | Must issue proper tax forms (W-2, 1099) |

*Quick Checklist: Foundational Deductions*

- ☑ Office supplies & software
- ☑ Phone & internet (business portion)
- ☑ Professional fees (CPA, attorney, consultant)
- ☑ Marketing, printing, and ads
- ☑ Business insurance premiums

## HOME OFFICE DEDUCTION

If you work from home, you can deduct the portion of your home used exclusively for business.

Two methods exist:

1. **Simplified method:** $5 per square foot, up to 300 sq ft (max $1,500).
2. **Regular method:** Based on actual expenses (utilities, mortgage interest, insurance, property taxes, etc.) multiplied by business-use percentage.

**Pro Tip:** *"Exclusive use" means exactly that. If your office doubles as a guest room, it doesn't qualify.*

**Avoid This Mistake:** Claiming an unrealistic percentage of your home. Stay conservative—between 10% – 20% is typical for most small home-based businesses.

## VEHICLE AND MILEAGE DEDUCTION

If you use your car for business, you can deduct either:

- **Standard mileage rate** (2025 rate ≈ 67 ¢ per mile, check annually), or
- **Actual expenses** (fuel, repairs, depreciation, insurance, etc.)

**Example:**

You drive 8,000 business miles this year.
8,000 × $0.67 = **$5,360 deduction.**

*Quick Checklist: Vehicle Deductions*

- ☑ Track mileage with an app (TripLog, MileIQ, Everlance)
- ☑ Record date, trip purpose, and miles driven
- ☑ Keep gas and maintenance receipts
- ☑ Log odometer readings at year-start and year-end

**Pro Tip:** *If your business vehicle is financed, interest is also deductible.*

**Avoid This Mistake:** Claiming 100% business use on a personal vehicle—rarely defensible. Split business vs. personal realistically.

## TRAVEL, MEALS & ENTERTAINMENT

**Travel** expenses include airfare, hotels, rental cars, taxis, and 50% of meals while away on business.

**Business meals** are 50% deductible if they are directly related to your business and involve a client, customer, or team meeting.

| Expense | Deductible? | Notes |
|---|---|---|
| Airfare, Lodging, Ground Transport | ☑ | Business purpose must be documented |
| Meals w/ Clients or Staff | ☑ (50%) | Keep who, where, and why noted |
| Entertainment (concerts, sports, etc.) | × | No longer deductible post-2018 |

**Pro Tip:** *Write the person's name and meeting purpose directly on your receipt right after the meal. It saves hours later.*

## EQUIPMENT & DEPRECIATION

Big-ticket purchases—computers, tools, vehicles, or furniture—can often be deducted immediately under **Section 179** or **bonus depreciation.**

| Method | Limit | Benefit |
|---|---|---|
| **Section 179** | Up to $1,220,000 (2025 est.) | Deduct full cost in year placed in service |
| **Bonus Depreciation** | 60% in 2025 | Deduct large portion of cost; rest depreciated |

**Example:**

You buy new equipment for $10,000.
If eligible, you may deduct the entire amount this year instead of spreading it over five years.

**Pro Tip:** *Work with your CPA to time major purchases. Buying in December vs. January can change which tax year benefits.*

## HEALTH INSURANCE & RETIREMENT

If you're self-employed, you can deduct **100% of health-insurance premiums** for yourself, your spouse, and dependents—provided you're not eligible for an employer plan.

Also consider **retirement plan deductions:**

- **SEP IRA:** Up to 25% of compensation (max ≈ $69,000 for 2025).
- **Solo 401(k):** Employee + employer contributions up to combined $76,500 (if age 50+).

> **Pro Tip:** *These deductions reduce both income and self-employment tax—making them some of the most powerful small-business tax tools.*

## GRAY AREAS AND RED FLAGS

Certain deductions are legal but often abused. These don't make them wrong—but they require solid documentation.

**Common Audit Triggers**

- Excessive meals or travel for a local business
- 100% vehicle use claims
- Large "miscellaneous" or "other" expense categories
- Home-office deduction without proof of exclusive use

> **Pro Tip:** *When in doubt, over-document. Keep receipts, notes, and calendar entries that clearly show business purpose.*

## WHAT YOU *CAN'T* DEDUCT

Not every expense is deductible—even if it feels "business related."

| Non-Deductible Expense | Reason |
|---|---|
| Personal groceries, clothing | Personal living expenses |
| Political contributions | Not business-related |
| Penalties, fines, or late fees | IRS disallows them |
| Commuting to your main office | Considered personal transportation |
| Gifts over $25 per recipient per year | Deduction limited by IRS rules |

**Avoid This Mistake:** Forgetting that personal spending through a business account can invalidate deductions. Keep personal and business separate.

## MAXIMIZING DEDUCTIONS THE RIGHT WAY

*Quick Checklist: Deduction Strategy*

- ☑ Keep separate business accounts & credit cards
- ☑ Categorize expenses monthly
- ☑ Save digital receipts for every deduction
- ☑ Track mileage & home-office space
- ☑ Review deductions quarterly with your CPA

**Pro Tip:** *Don't aim to "pay zero taxes." Aim to* **pay fair taxes on real profit***—while keeping every legitimate deduction you deserve.*

## KEY TAKEAWAY

Every dollar you can prove as a business expense is one less dollar taxed. The goal isn't to outsmart the IRS—it's to **operate with wisdom and precision.**

Strong recordkeeping and thoughtful deduction planning transform tax season from panic to progress.

Next up:
**Chapter 5 – Home Office, Vehicles & Travel**
→ A deeper look at specific deductions—how to calculate them correctly, keep compliant records, and avoid red flags.

*Chapter 5*

# Home Office, Vehicles & Travel

*How to Maximize Everyday Deductions Without Inviting IRS Trouble*

Most small business owners use their home, their car, and occasional travel for business purposes—but few take full advantage of the tax benefits available.

These are some of the **most misunderstood** areas of the tax code, and the ones most likely to either save you thousands—or cause problems if done wrong.

This chapter will help you get it right, confidently.

## THE HOME OFFICE DEDUCTION — SIMPLIFIED

If you work from home, you may be eligible for one of the most powerful deductions available: the **home office deduction.**

The key is that the space must be used **regularly and exclusively** for business.

**Two Ways to Claim It**

| Method | How It Works | Best For |
|---|---|---|
| **Simplified Method** | $5 per square foot, up to 300 sq. ft. (max $1,500) | Simplicity and smaller spaces |
| **Actual Expense Method** | Deducts a percentage of actual home expenses | Larger or high-cost homes |

To use the actual-expense method, calculate the square footage of your office divided by your home's total area. Multiply that percentage by qualifying home costs such as mortgage interest, rent, utilities, repairs, and insurance.

**Example:**

You use a 200 sq. ft. office in a 2,000 sq. ft. home → 10%.
If your annual utilities and rent total $24,000, you can deduct **$2,400 (10%)** as a home-office expense.

**Pro Tip:** *Even a small dedicated space counts—a spare bedroom, garage studio, or finished basement can qualify if it's exclusive to business use.*

**Avoid This Mistake:** Claiming your kitchen table or shared living area. The IRS disallows spaces used for both personal and business purposes.

*Quick Checklist: Home Office Compliance*

- ☑ Space used regularly and exclusively for business
- ☑ Clear business-use photos or floorplan on file
- ☑ Expenses documented and stored with receipts
- ☑ Renters include portion of rent & utilities
- ☑ Homeowners include mortgage interest, insurance, and depreciation

## BUSINESS USE OF YOUR VEHICLE

If you drive for business purposes, part of your vehicle expenses may be deductible.

The key is separating **personal** miles from **business** miles.

**Qualifying Trips Include:**

- Visiting clients or vendors
- Driving between job sites
- Picking up supplies
- Business-related banking or post office runs
- Attending networking or industry events

**Non-Qualifying Trips Include:**

- Commuting from home to your main office
- Personal errands during business trips
- Driving family members to non-business locations

## TWO METHODS FOR DEDUCTING VEHICLE USE

| Method | Description | When to Use |
|---|---|---|
| **Standard Mileage Rate** | Multiply business miles × IRS mileage rate (≈ 67¢/mile for 2025) | Easy tracking, lighter vehicle use |
| **Actual Expense Method** | Deduct % of gas, maintenance, depreciation, insurance | Better for high-cost or business-only vehicles |

**Example:**

You drive 10,000 business miles in 2025.
10,000 × $0.67 = **$6,700 deduction.**

**Pro Tip:** *Use a mileage-tracking app (MileIQ, Everlance, or QuickBooks Mileage) to automatically log trips. The IRS accepts digital mileage logs.*

**Avoid This Mistake:** Claiming "100% business use" unless it's a dedicated company vehicle. Even small personal errands can invalidate full deductions.

*Quick Checklist: Vehicle Deduction Prep*

- ☑ Record odometer readings on Jan 1 and Dec 31
- ☑ Track each trip's date, purpose, and miles
- ☑ Keep gas, maintenance, and insurance receipts
- ☑ Document percentage of business use
- ☑ Review with CPA before claiming large write-offs

**Pro Tip:** *If your business owns the vehicle, title it under your company name and pay all related expenses through the business account.*

## TRAVEL EXPENSES: DEDUCTING BUSINESS TRIPS

Business travel can be highly deductible—as long as your **primary purpose** is business, not personal vacation.

**What Qualifies as Business Travel?**

- Attending conferences or seminars
- Meeting clients or partners
- Exploring expansion or investment opportunities
- Visiting remote job sites or suppliers

If your trip is primarily for business, you can deduct:

- Airfare or mileage
- Hotels and lodging
- Taxis, rideshare, or car rentals
- 50% of meals while traveling
- Internet and phone costs
- Shipping or baggage fees

**Example:**

You attend a 3-day conference in Dallas.

Airfare: $400, Hotel: $600, Meals: $180 (50% deductible), Taxi: $120 → Total deductible = $1,270.

> **Pro Tip:** *Keep a printed itinerary, event registration, and receipts. If the trip includes personal days, document business vs. personal time.*

**Avoid This Mistake:** Mixing too much leisure into a "business" trip. The IRS allows reasonable downtime, but if business isn't the primary motive, deductions can be denied.

## MIXING BUSINESS AND FAMILY TRAVEL

Can you combine a family vacation with business? Yes—but be careful.

You may deduct **only** the expenses directly related to the business portion.

**Example:**

You attend a 2-day client meeting in Orlando and then stay 3 more days for family vacation.

- Airfare: 100% deductible (business was primary purpose)
- Lodging: 2/5 deductible (2 of 5 days were business)
- Meals: 50% deductible for business days only

**Pro Tip:** *If your spouse travels with you, their costs are deductible only if they are an employee and their presence serves a business purpose.*

## LOCAL TRAVEL AND COMMUTING

Local business errands are deductible as mileage or actual vehicle costs, but **commuting from home to your regular office** is *not.*

However, if your home qualifies as your principal place of business, then travel from your home to clients or job sites *is* deductible.

*Quick Checklist: Local Travel*

- ☑ Track local trips like client meetings and supply runs
- ☑ Keep a simple log of dates, miles, and purposes
- ☑ Separate commuting from true business trips

**Pro Tip:** *A qualifying home office can turn your daily drive into a deductible business trip.*

## MEALS DURING TRAVEL

While on business trips, **50% of meals** are deductible if they're not lavish and are directly related to your work.

| Meal Type | Deductible? | Notes |
|---|---|---|
| Meal with client during trip | ☑ 50% | Must discuss business |
| Meal alone while traveling | ☑ 50% | Away from home overnight |
| Family meal during mixed trip | × | Personal portion disallowed |
| Entertainment (concerts, golf, etc.) | × | No longer deductible |

**Pro Tip:** *Write the person's name, business discussed, and date on the receipt immediately. It creates a built-in audit trail.*

## RECORDKEEPING FOR TRAVEL

*Quick Checklist: Business Travel Documentation*

- ☑ Keep all receipts for airfare, hotels, and ground transport
- ☑ Retain event tickets, itineraries, and meeting notes
- ☑ Record dates, destinations, and business purposes
- ☑ Track meals separately (50% rule)
- ☑ Store scanned copies in a "Travel Expenses" folder by year

**Avoid This Mistake:** Losing receipts or waiting until tax time to reconstruct travel records. The IRS requires contemporaneous evidence—write it down while it's fresh.

## BRINGING IT ALL TOGETHER

Your home, vehicle, and travel costs are part of running a modern business. When used correctly—and documented properly—they provide legitimate, significant tax savings every year.

**Pro Tip:** *The key isn't creativity—it's consistency. Keep good records, make honest allocations, and consult your CPA before claiming large deductions.*

## QUICK RECAP: THE SMART DEDUCTION FORMULA

| Category | Typical Deduction | Documentation Needed |
|---|---|---|
| **Home Office** | 10–20% of home expenses | Floorplan, receipts, photos |
| **Vehicle Use** | 67¢/mile or % of expenses | Mileage log, receipts |
| **Business Travel** | 100% travel costs, 50% meals | Receipts, itinerary, notes |
| **Mixed Trips** | Business portion only | Document days & purposes |

Next up:

**Chapter 6 – Hiring, Payroll & Contractor Taxes**

→ How to properly pay yourself and others, handle 1099s and W-2s, and avoid IRS penalties while building a growing team.

*Chapter 6*

# Hiring, Payroll & Contractor Taxes

*How to Pay Yourself and Others the Smart, Compliant Way*

As your business grows, you'll reach a pivotal moment: you can't do it all yourself anymore. That's when you begin **hiring help**—and with that comes new tax responsibilities.

Whether you bring on employees, independent contractors, or just start paying yourself regularly, understanding how payroll taxes work is critical to keeping your business compliant and profitable.

## THE THREE WAYS OWNERS GET PAID

Depending on your business structure, there are different ways to legally take money out of your company:

| Entity Type | Owner Compensation | Tax Impact |
|---|---|---|
| **Sole Proprietor / Single-Member LLC** | Owner's draw | Subject to self-employment tax |
| **Partnership / Multi-Member LLC** | Partner distributions | Self-employment tax on earnings |
| **S-Corporation** | Reasonable salary (W-2) + distributions | Salary subject to payroll tax; distributions are not |
| **C-Corporation** | W-2 salary + dividends | Salary taxed as income, dividends taxed again at shareholder level |

**Pro Tip:** *If your business is profitable and structured as an LLC, discuss* **S-Corp election** *with your CPA—it can save thousands in self-employment taxes each year.*

## HIRING HELP: EMPLOYEE VS. INDEPENDENT CONTRACTOR

One of the most common—and costly—mistakes small business owners make is **misclassifying workers.**

**Employee (W-2)**

- You control *how*, *when*, and *where* they work.
- You provide tools, training, and supervision.
- You must withhold and pay payroll taxes.

**Independent Contractor (1099)**

- They control *how* the job gets done.
- They provide their own tools and set their own schedule.
- You pay the total invoice—no withholdings.

**Example:**
If you pay a contractor $2,000 for a project, they handle their own taxes.

If you pay an employee $2,000, your total cost might be closer to **$2,300–$2,400** after employer payroll taxes.

**Avoid This Mistake:** Calling someone a "contractor" just to skip payroll taxes. The IRS can reclassify them and assess back taxes, penalties, and interest.

*Quick Checklist: Worker Classification*

- ☑ Who controls the work schedule and methods?
- ☑ Who provides tools/equipment?
- ☑ Is the worker offering the same services to others?
- ☑ Is the relationship ongoing or project-based?
- ☑ Review the IRS "Common Law Test" (20 factors) if unsure

**Pro Tip:** *Use a simple written contract for every contractor relationship—it clarifies terms and protects you both.*

## PAYROLL BASICS EVERY OWNER SHOULD KNOW

If you have employees, you must handle:

1. **Withholding payroll taxes** (Social Security, Medicare, income tax)
2. **Paying employer taxes** (matching Social Security & Medicare + unemployment)
3. **Filing payroll reports** (quarterly and annually)

| Tax Type | Who Pays It | Rate (Approx.) |
|---|---|---|
| **Social Security (OASDI)** | Both employer & employee | 6.2% each (12.4% total) |
| **Medicare (HI)** | Both employer & employee | 1.45% each (2.9% total) |
| **Federal Unemployment (FUTA)** | Employer only | 0.6% on first $7,000 wages |
| **State Unemployment (SUTA)** | Employer only | Varies by state |

**Pro Tip:** *Use payroll software (Gusto, QuickBooks Payroll, ADP, or Patriot) to automate filings and payments—it's inexpensive insurance against costly mistakes.*

## PAYING YOURSELF AS THE OWNER

If you're an **S-Corporation owner**, you're required to pay yourself a **reasonable salary** through payroll.

This means:

- Withhold and remit taxes just like any employee.
- Issue yourself a W-2 at year-end.
- Take remaining profit as distributions (no payroll tax).

**Example:**
Your S-Corp earns $120,000.

You pay yourself a $70,000 salary and take $50,000 as a distribution.
→ You save roughly **$7,500–$9,000** in self-employment taxes compared to a standard LLC.

**Avoid This Mistake:** Paying *no* salary as an S-Corp owner. The IRS routinely audits for this issue and can reclassify all distributions as taxable wages.

**Pro Tip:** *"Reasonable salary" means what you'd pay someone else to do your job in your region and industry—your CPA can benchmark this easily.*

## FORMS AND FILINGS YOU MUST KNOW

| Form | Purpose | Due Date |
|---|---|---|
| **W-4** | Employee withholding elections | At hire |
| **W-9** | Contractor info (EIN/SSN) | Before payment |
| **W-2** | Employee annual wage report | Jan 31 |
| **1099-NEC** | Contractor annual payment report | Jan 31 |
| **Form 941** | Quarterly payroll tax return | Quarterly |
| **Form 940** | Annual unemployment report | Jan 31 |

*Quick Checklist: Payroll Setup*

- ☑ Apply for EIN (if not done already)
- ☑ Register for state withholding & unemployment accounts
- ☑ Set up payroll software or service
- ☑ Collect W-4/W-9 from all workers
- ☑ File 941 & remit payroll taxes quarterly
- ☑ Send W-2s and 1099s by January 31 each year

**Pro Tip:** *If you pay any individual contractor* **$600 or more in a year,** *you must issue them a* **Form 1099-NEC.**

## PAYROLL FREQUENCY & CASH FLOW PLANNING

Most small businesses pay on one of three schedules:

- **Weekly** (great for labor-heavy industries)
- **Biweekly** (common for growing firms)

- **Monthly** (typical for owner-only S-Corps)

> **Pro Tip:** *Align payroll timing with your cash flow cycle—if clients pay monthly, don't schedule weekly payrolls.*

**Avoid This Mistake:** Missing payroll tax deposits. The IRS imposes heavy penalties (2–15% of the unpaid amount) and will pursue personally responsible owners.

## CONTRACTOR PAYMENTS SIMPLIFIED

Contractors simplify your payroll but still require proper documentation:

- Collect **W-9** before payment.
- Track total payments annually.
- Issue **Form 1099-NEC** by January 31.

**Example:**

If you pay a designer $1,200, a web developer $800, and a copywriter $2,000—all 1099s must be issued the next January.
Your business deducts the expense, and they report the income.

> **Pro Tip:** *If paying through a third-party platform (PayPal, Upwork, etc.), those companies may issue a 1099-K instead—check before duplicating forms.*

## HIRING FAMILY MEMBERS

Hiring your spouse or children can provide both tax and family benefits—when done correctly.

| Family Member | Rules & Benefits |
|---|---|
| **Spouse** | Can be paid wages; qualifies for retirement contributions and Social Security credits |
| **Children (under 18)** | Wages not subject to Social Security or Medicare if business is parent-owned sole prop or LLC |
| **Children (over 18)** | Regular payroll taxes apply, but still deductible to the business |

**Pro Tip:** *Hiring your kids for legitimate work (like marketing, inventory, or admin) can shift income into lower tax brackets—just keep time sheets and pay reasonable wages.*

**Avoid This Mistake:** Claiming family payroll without real work performed. Documentation is everything.

## OUTSOURCING PAYROLL: WHEN IT'S WORTH IT

Once you have even one employee (or yourself on S-Corp payroll), outsourcing payroll can be a huge time-saver.

Benefits include:

- Automatic filings and deposits
- Compliance monitoring for deadlines
- Employee portals for pay stubs and W-2s
- Integration with bookkeeping systems

*Quick Checklist: Payroll Provider Selection*

- ☑ Confirm they handle tax filings and deposits
- ☑ Review fees (monthly + per-employee)
- ☑ Ask about workers' comp integration
- ☑ Ensure they provide annual W-2s/1099s
- ☑ Verify they are bonded and insured

**Pro Tip:** *Even one missed payroll filing can cost more than a year's worth of payroll service fees.*

## BRINGING IT ALL TOGETHER

Hiring help is a major milestone—it means your business is growing. But it also means stepping into new tax territory.

With clear systems, accurate classifications, and professional payroll tools, you'll build confidence, protect your business, and keep the IRS happy.

### Quick Recap Checklist

- ☑ Classify workers correctly (W-2 vs. 1099)
- ☑ Set up payroll and file quarterly reports
- ☑ Issue W-2s/1099s by January 31
- ☑ Pay yourself a reasonable salary (S-Corp)
- ☑ Keep documentation for every payment

**Pro Tip:** *Payroll is about stewardship—doing right by your people, your business, and your future self.*

Next up:

**Chapter 7 – Quarterly Taxes & Cash Flow**

→ Learn how to estimate, save, and pay quarterly taxes like a pro—without the year-end panic.

*Chapter 7*

# Quarterly Taxes & Cash Flow

*How to Stay Ahead of the IRS and Keep More Cash in Your Business*

Nothing drains a small business owner's joy faster than an unexpected tax bill.

That sinking feeling in April—realizing you owe thousands more than you thought—is entirely avoidable with one simple discipline: **quarterly tax planning.**

When you understand how estimated taxes work and build them into your cash flow rhythm, you'll stay compliant, eliminate surprises, and keep your business financially strong all year long.

## WHY QUARTERLY TAXES EXIST

If you're self-employed or own a business that doesn't withhold taxes from your pay, the IRS expects you to pay income and self-employment taxes **as you earn money**—not just once a year.

That's why they created **estimated quarterly payments**: four installments throughout the year that cover your income and self-employment tax obligations.

| Quarter | Period Covered | Due Date |
|---|---|---|
| Q1 | Jan 1 – Mar 31 | April 15 |
| Q2 | Apr 1 – May 31 | June 15 |
| Q3 | Jun 1 – Aug 31 | Sept 15 |
| Q4 | Sep 1 – Dec 31 | Jan 15 (next year) |

**Pro Tip:** *Mark these four dates on your calendar now—and set up automatic reminders. Consistency beats scrambling every April.*

## HOW TO ESTIMATE WHAT YOU OWE

The simplest method: **Estimate your annual profit**, multiply by your estimated tax rate, and divide by four.

**Example:**
You expect to earn $80,000 net income this year.
Estimated combined tax rate (federal + state + SE tax) ≈ 25%.
$80,000 × 25% = $20,000 total taxes → $5,000 per quarter.

*Quick Checklist: Quarterly Tax Formula*

- ☑ Project your annual income and expenses
- ☑ Calculate expected profit (income – expenses)
- ☑ Multiply by combined tax rate (usually 20–30%)
- ☑ Divide by four to get quarterly payment amount
- ☑ Adjust mid-year if income changes significantly

**Pro Tip:** *If your business income fluctuates seasonally, use the* **annualized income method** *(IRS Form 2210) to pay less in slow quarters and more when business picks up.*

## HOW TO MAKE PAYMENTS

You can pay quarterly taxes easily online:

- **IRS Direct Pay:** www.irs.gov/payments/direct-pay
- **EFTPS (Electronic Federal Tax Payment System):** www.eftps.gov
- **State Payments:** via your state's Department of Revenue website

**Pro Tip:** *Use EFTPS if you want confirmation history and automatic scheduling—perfect for disciplined business owners.*

**Avoid This Mistake:** Paying estimated taxes from your **personal account.** Always pay from your business account to keep clean records.

## UNDERSTANDING SELF-EMPLOYMENT TAX

Self-employment tax covers **Social Security and Medicare**—the same taxes employees and employers split through payroll.

As a business owner, you pay both halves yourself (15.3% total).

| Component | Rate | Applies To |
|---|---|---|
| Social Security | 12.4% | First $168,600 (2025) |
| Medicare | 2.9% | All earnings + 0.9% surtax over $200k (single) |

**Pro Tip:** *If you elect S-Corp status and pay yourself a salary, only your W-2 wages are subject to payroll tax—***distributions are not.** *This is one of the most effective small-business tax planning tools.*

## INTEGRATING TAXES INTO YOUR CASH FLOW

The best tax plan isn't about calculations—it's about **habit.**

Set up a system that makes saving for taxes automatic and stress-free.

### The "Profit First" Method (Simplified)

1. Open a separate **Tax Savings Account.**
2. Transfer a fixed percentage of all revenue (e.g., 25%) into it weekly.
3. Use that account exclusively for quarterly and annual tax payments.

**Example:**
If your business brings in $10,000 this month and you transfer 25% to taxes, you'll have $2,500 ready when payments are due.

No surprises, no scrambling.

*Quick Checklist: Cash Flow System*

- ☑ Open dedicated tax savings account
- ☑ Choose a fixed transfer percentage (start with 25%)
- ☑ Transfer automatically with every deposit
- ☑ Review account balance before each quarterly deadline
- ☑ Never "borrow" from your tax account

**Pro Tip:** *If cash flow is tight, start smaller (10–15%) and gradually increase. Progress matters more than perfection.*

## AVOIDING PENALTIES

If you underpay your taxes during the year, the IRS can charge **underpayment penalties**—even if you pay everything by April 15.

To avoid them, meet one of these **safe harbor rules:**

1. Pay at least **90% of your current-year tax**, OR
2. Pay **100% of your previous-year tax** (110% if prior-year income > $150,000).

**Pro Tip:** *If you had a high-profit year followed by a slower one, using the "90% current-year" rule usually saves money. If your income is rising, "100% prior-year" is safer.*

**Avoid This Mistake:** Confusing *profit* with *cash flow*. You might have plenty of revenue but no liquidity for taxes if you overspend on operations.

## WHEN TO ADJUST YOUR QUARTERLY PAYMENTS

Review your financials mid-year or anytime your income changes significantly—especially if:

- You add new revenue streams
- You hire employees
- You make a large equipment purchase
- You elect S-Corp status mid-year

Your CPA can run a **mid-year tax projection** to fine-tune your next payments and prevent over- or under-paying.

*Quick Checklist: Mid-Year Tax Review*

- ☑ Update your bookkeeping through June 30
- ☑ Review net profit YTD
- ☑ Estimate full-year projection
- ☑ Adjust remaining quarterly payments accordingly
- ☑ Revisit tax savings percentage if needed

## HANDLING MULTI-STATE OR LOCAL TAXES

If you do business in multiple states, you may owe **state income tax** in each location where you have *nexus* (a physical or economic presence).

**Pro Tip:** *If you sell online or across state lines, discuss nexus rules with your CPA. Each state has its own thresholds for when you owe tax.*

**Avoid This Mistake:** Ignoring state filing requirements for remote contractors or sales—it's one of the most common triggers for state tax notices.

## CASH FLOW MINDSET: PAYING TAXES WITH CONFIDENCE

Paying taxes isn't just compliance—it's part of running a healthy business.

Owners who plan ahead experience less stress, make better decisions, and sleep better at night knowing they're ready for every deadline.

**Pro Tip:** *Think of your tax payments as "investing in peace of mind." You're not losing money—you're protecting your integrity, credibility, and sanity.*

*Quick Recap Checklist*

- ☑ Mark quarterly deadlines on your calendar
- ☑ Calculate payments using 25–30% of profit
- ☑ Use a dedicated tax savings account
- ☑ Pay through IRS Direct Pay or EFTPS
- ☑ Review mid-year with your CPA

## KEY TAKEAWAY

Quarterly taxes are not a punishment—they're a rhythm.

When you turn tax planning into a monthly habit, you'll never dread April again. Your business will run smoothly, your cash flow will stay steady, and you'll build lasting financial confidence.

Next up:
**Chapter 8 – Retirement Plans & Benefits**
→ Discover how to build wealth for yourself and your team through tax-advantaged retirement plans and smart benefit strategies.

*Chapter 8*

# Retirement Plans & Benefits

*Building Wealth for Yourself and Your Team While Reducing Taxes*

Owning a small business gives you freedom and flexibility—but it also means you're responsible for your own retirement.

Unlike employees who rely on company plans, business owners must intentionally build their future security.

The good news? The tax code rewards you for doing it.

Smart retirement and benefit planning can lower your tax bill today while funding long-term wealth tomorrow.

## WHY RETIREMENT PLANNING MATTERS FOR ENTREPRENEURS

Many small business owners reinvest every dollar back into their company, assuming they'll "catch up later."

But without a structured plan, "later" rarely happens.

Retirement savings are one of the few ways to:

- Grow wealth tax-deferred or tax-free
- Reduce taxable income each year
- Prepare for an eventual business exit

**Pro Tip:** *Think of retirement contributions as part of your tax strategy, not just your future plan. Every dollar you invest could lower this year's taxable income.*

## CHOOSING THE RIGHT RETIREMENT PLAN

Let's look at the most common and powerful options for small business owners.

| Plan Type | Contribution Limit (2025 est.) | Who It's For | Key Benefits |
|---|---|---|---|
| **Traditional IRA** | $7,000 ($8,000 if 50+) | Any individual with income | Easy setup, tax-deductible contributions |
| **Roth IRA** | $7,000 ($8,000 if 50+) | Income limits apply | Tax-free withdrawals in retirement |
| **SEP IRA** | Up to 25% of comp, max $69,000 | Solo or small biz with few employees | High limit, flexible annual funding |
| **Solo 401(k)** | Up to $76,500 (with catch-up) | Self-employed or owner-only | Highest flexibility, pre- and post-tax options |
| **SIMPLE IRA** | $16,000 + $3,500 catch-up | Small biz under 100 employees | Employer match up to 3%, easy to administer |
| **401(k) (Traditional)** | $23,000 + $7,500 catch-up | Larger businesses with staff | Employee benefit, strong retention tool |

### 1. SEP IRA (Simplified Employee Pension)

The **SEP IRA** is one of the easiest and most flexible retirement options for small business owners.

You can contribute up to **25% of your compensation** (net profit if self-employed), up to a maximum of about **$69,000 (2025)**.

**Advantages:**

- Easy to set up and maintain
- No required annual contributions
- Can contribute after year-end (before tax filing deadline)

**Pro Tip:** *You can open and fund a SEP IRA as late as your tax filing deadline, including extensions—making it a powerful year-end tax planning tool.*

**Avoid This Mistake:** If you have employees, you must contribute the **same percentage** for them as you do for yourself. A 25% owner contribution = 25% for all eligible employees.

**2. Solo 401(k) – The Powerhouse Plan**

A **Solo 401(k)** (also called an Individual 401(k)) offers higher contribution limits and flexibility for self-employed owners with no employees (except a spouse).

You can contribute in two ways:

- **Employee contribution:** up to $23,000 ($30,500 if 50+)
- **Employer contribution:** up to 25% of net profit
  → Combined limit up to **$76,500** (2025).

**Advantages:**

- Highest contribution potential of any small-biz plan
- Can include Roth (after-tax) and Traditional (pre-tax) options
- Can take loans (up to $50,000 or 50% of balance)

**Pro Tip:** *You must open a Solo 401(k) by* **December 31** *of the tax year to qualify—though you can fund it until your filing deadline.*

**Avoid This Mistake:** Missing the setup deadline. A SEP can be opened later, but a Solo 401(k) cannot—it must exist before year-end.

**3. SIMPLE IRA**

The **SIMPLE IRA** (Savings Incentive Match Plan for Employees) is perfect for businesses with fewer than 100 employees who want an easy, affordable plan with a built-in match.

- Employees can contribute up to **$16,000** annually.
- Employers match up to **3% of pay** or contribute a flat 2% for all eligible employees.

**Advantages:**

- Easy to administer (no annual 5500 filing)
- Encourages employee participation
- Reduces taxable income for both employer and employee

**Pro Tip:** *SIMPLE IRAs must be established by* **October 1** *of the year you want to start contributing.*

#### 4. Traditional and Roth IRAs

Even if you have a business retirement plan, you can often still contribute to **personal IRAs** (depending on income limits).

| Type | Tax Treatment | When You Pay Taxes |
|---|---|---|
| **Traditional IRA** | Deduct now, taxed later | Withdrawals in retirement |
| **Roth IRA** | Pay now, tax-free later | No tax on qualified withdrawals |

**Pro Tip:** *Diversify your tax future—combine pre-tax (Traditional) and post-tax (Roth) savings for flexibility in retirement.*

## ADDING HEALTH AND FRINGE BENEFITS

Beyond retirement, offering (or structuring) benefits can reduce your taxable income while providing value to you and your team.

#### Health Insurance

- **Self-employed?** Deduct 100% of your health insurance premiums for yourself, your spouse, and dependents (if not covered by another employer plan).
- **S-Corp Owners:** If the business pays your premiums, they are deductible by the company and included as W-2 income—but you can still deduct them personally.

#### Health Savings Account (HSA)

If you have a **high-deductible health plan (HDHP)**, you can contribute to an HSA—one of the few **triple-tax-advantaged** accounts:

1. Contributions are tax-deductible.
2. Growth is tax-free.
3. Withdrawals for medical expenses are tax-free.

| 2025 Contribution Limits | Individual | Family |
|---|---|---|
| HSA | $4,300 | $8,550 |
| Catch-Up (age 55+) | +$1,000 | +$1,000 |

**Pro Tip:** *Treat your HSA like a "medical retirement account." Pay small medical bills out of pocket and let the HSA grow tax-free for decades.*

## EMPLOYEE BENEFITS THAT ALSO HELP YOU

Offering benefits isn't just generous—it's strategic.

They can reduce turnover, boost morale, and lower your taxable income.

*Quick Checklist: Smart Small-Business Benefits*

- ☑ Retirement plan contributions (SEP, SIMPLE, 401(k))
- ☑ Health insurance premiums
- ☑ HSA or FSA programs
- ☑ Education reimbursements
- ☑ Cell phone or internet stipends
- ☑ Wellness benefits (gym, counseling, etc.)

**Pro Tip:** *Many benefits are 100% deductible to your business and often tax-free to employees—a win-win.*

## INTEGRATING RETIREMENT INTO YOUR TAX PLAN

Your retirement plan is not separate from your tax strategy—it's part of it.

Think of it as shifting money from **"tax now"** to **"tax later."**

**Example:**
You earn $100,000 net income.
You contribute $20,000 to a SEP IRA.

You now pay taxes on **$80,000 instead of $100,000.**
At a 25% tax rate, that's **$5,000 saved** this year—plus long-term investment growth.

**Pro Tip:** *Even modest annual contributions compound dramatically. A $10,000 annual investment earning 7% will exceed* **$1 million in 30 years.**

## WHEN TO HIRE HELP

If your business grows beyond one or two employees, consider hiring:

- A **retirement plan administrator** to manage filings and compliance.
- A **CPA or financial advisor** to coordinate contributions and ensure IRS limits are met.

*Quick Checklist: Setting Up a Plan*

- ☑ Choose your ideal plan (SEP, Solo 401(k), SIMPLE, or full 401(k))
- ☑ Open account by required deadline
- ☑ Fund contributions before filing deadline
- ☑ Maintain records of contributions and matching
- ☑ Review annually with your CPA

**Avoid This Mistake:** Neglecting to review plan limits annually. The IRS updates them almost every year—don't miss out on higher savings potential.

## KEY TAKEAWAY

Smart entrepreneurs don't wait until "someday" to plan their retirement—they integrate it into their tax and business strategy now.

Every contribution builds wealth, reduces taxes, and reinforces your long-term financial foundation.

**Pro Tip:** *The best retirement plan is the one you'll actually fund. Start small, stay consistent, and increase as your business grows.*

Next up:
**Chapter 9 – Tax Credits You Might Be Missing**
→ A look at often-overlooked small-business tax credits—from R&D to energy incentives—and how to qualify for them.

*Chapter 9*

# Tax Credits You Might Be Missing

*Hidden Incentives That Can Save Small Businesses Thousands*

Tax **deductions** lower your *taxable income.*

Tax **credits** reduce your *tax bill dollar for dollar.*

That difference is huge. A $1,000 deduction might save you $250 in taxes. A $1,000 credit saves you the full $1,000.

Yet many small business owners never claim the credits available to them—either because they don't know they exist or assume they're only for big corporations.

Let's fix that.

## WHAT IS A TAX CREDIT?

A **tax credit** is an incentive written into the tax code to encourage certain business behaviors—like hiring, innovation, or investing in clean energy.

There are two main types:

- **Nonrefundable credits**: Can reduce your tax bill to zero, but not below.
- **Refundable credits**: Can create a refund even if your tax owed is already zero.

**Pro Tip:** *Always check whether a credit is refundable or nonrefundable. Refundable credits (like some energy and health-care credits) can yield cash back.*

## COMMON SMALL BUSINESS TAX CREDITS

Here are the top credits that often go overlooked by small business owners:

| Credit Name | Typical Benefit | Best For |
|---|---|---|
| **Research & Development (R&D)** | 6–10% of qualifying expenses | Innovative service or product companies |
| **Work Opportunity Tax Credit (WOTC)** | Up to $9,600 per eligible hire | Businesses hiring from targeted groups |
| **Disabled Access Credit** | Up to $5,000 | Businesses making facilities ADA-compliant |
| **Energy-Efficient Property Credit** | 30% of qualifying solar or clean-energy costs | Businesses installing renewable systems |
| **Small Employer Health Insurance Credit** | Up to 50% of premiums paid | Employers with ≤25 employees providing insurance |
| **Startup Costs for Retirement Plans** | Up to $5,000 per year | Businesses starting a SEP, SIMPLE, or 401(k) |
| **Family & Medical Leave Credit** | 12.5–25% of wages paid | Employers offering paid family leave |

Let's unpack the most relevant ones for small business owners.

## 1. RESEARCH & DEVELOPMENT (R&D) TAX CREDIT

Despite its name, you don't need a laboratory to qualify.

If you're improving a product, process, or technology—even software or internal systems—you may be eligible.

Qualifying activities include:

- Developing or improving software
- Creating new prototypes or formulas

- Streamlining manufacturing or production
- Experimenting with new materials or designs

**Example:**
A small tech firm spends $50,000 improving its internal app.
They may qualify for a **$5,000–$7,000 R&D tax credit**—directly reducing their taxes owed.

> **Pro Tip:** *The R&D credit can often be applied against* **payroll taxes** *for startups under five years old.*

**Avoid This Mistake:** Failing to document your process. Keep notes, versions, and invoices—proof of "experimentation" is key to claiming this credit.

## 2. WORK OPPORTUNITY TAX CREDIT (WOTC)

The **WOTC** rewards businesses for hiring individuals from certain groups that face employment barriers, including:

- Veterans
- Ex-felons
- Long-term unemployed
- SNAP (food assistance) recipients
- Individuals living in empowerment zones

The credit ranges from **$2,400 up to $9,600 per qualified employee**, depending on category and hours worked.

*Quick Checklist: WOTC Steps*

- ☑ Have new hires complete IRS Form 8850 on or before their start date
- ☑ Submit to your state workforce agency within 28 days
- ☑ Keep certification documents for your records

**Pro Tip:** *Even one qualifying employee can offset thousands in taxes. Many payroll services (like ADP or Paychex) can handle WOTC screening automatically.*

## 3. DISABLED ACCESS CREDIT

If you spend money making your business accessible for customers or employees with disabilities, you can receive a **credit up to $5,000** (50% of qualifying costs between $250 and $10,250).

Examples include:

- Installing ramps, automatic doors, or elevators
- Upgrading restrooms for ADA compliance
- Providing accessible software or equipment

**Pro Tip:** *This credit is especially useful for service-based businesses that retrofit offices or retail spaces.*

**Avoid This Mistake:** Confusing this credit with a deduction. Credits are applied *after* calculating taxable income—they're far more valuable.

## 4. ENERGY-EFFICIENT AND CLEAN-ENERGY CREDITS

If your business invests in **solar panels, electric vehicles, or energy-efficient upgrades**, you may qualify for credits under the **Inflation Reduction Act (IRA)** and related energy programs.

| Type | Typical Credit | Notes |
|---|---|---|
| **Solar energy systems** | 30% of total cost | Includes installation and labor |
| **EV (Electric Vehicle) purchases** | Up to $7,500 per vehicle | Must meet specific battery & assembly standards |
| **Commercial building improvements** | $2.50–$5.00 per sq. ft. | Energy-efficient HVAC, lighting, insulation |

**Pro Tip:** *Keep manufacturer certification statements and invoices. Credits require documentation showing compliance with IRS standards.*

## 5. SMALL EMPLOYER HEALTH INSURANCE CREDIT

If you provide health insurance to your employees, you may qualify for a **credit up to 50%** of premiums paid through the **Small Business Health Options Program (SHOP)**.

Requirements:

- Fewer than 25 full-time employees
- Average wages under about $65,000 per year
- Employer pays at least 50% of premiums

**Example:**

If you pay $24,000 toward staff health insurance, the credit could save you **up to $12,000** directly against your tax bill.

> **Pro Tip:** *This credit can be claimed for* **two consecutive years**, *so plan strategically when you start offering coverage.*

## 6. RETIREMENT PLAN STARTUP CREDIT

The government rewards you for helping employees (and yourself) save for retirement.

If you start a new **401(k), SEP, or SIMPLE IRA**, you can receive a credit for **50% of setup and admin costs**, up to **$5,000 per year for three years.**

An additional $500 credit is available for including automatic enrollment features.

*Quick Checklist: Retirement Credit*

- ☑ Establish plan by year-end
- ☑ Have at least one employee (non-owner) participating
- ☑ File IRS Form 8881 to claim the credit

**Pro Tip:** *Combine this with your deductible retirement contributions for a double benefit: lower taxes now and in the future.*

## 7. FAMILY AND MEDICAL LEAVE CREDIT

If you voluntarily offer **paid family or medical leave** to employees, you may qualify for a credit between **12.5% and 25%** of wages paid during leave.

Requirements:

- Written policy providing at least two weeks of paid leave
- Employees must receive at least 50% of normal wages during leave
- Applies to both full-time and part-time staff

**Pro Tip:** *This credit is available through 2025 (subject to renewal)—check each year to confirm continuation.*

## COMBINING CREDITS STRATEGICALLY

You can often combine multiple credits in one year—as long as they apply to different expenses.

**Example:**

A business installs solar panels ($9,000 credit), starts a SIMPLE IRA ($2,500 credit), and hires a qualified veteran ($4,000 WOTC).
→ Total potential tax savings = **$15,500**.

**Avoid This Mistake:** Double-dipping—claiming both a credit and a deduction for the same expense. The IRS requires you to reduce your deduction by the credit amount claimed.

**Pro Tip:** *Credits can be carried forward for future years if they exceed your current tax liability. Always track unused credits with your CPA.*

## YOUR NEXT STEP

*Quick Checklist: Claiming Tax Credits*

- ☑ Review this list annually with your CPA
- ☑ Identify eligible hiring, energy, or benefit activities
- ☑ Complete required IRS forms (8850, 8881, 3800, etc.)
- ☑ Keep certification and receipts
- ☑ Track any carryforward credits for future years

**Pro Tip:** *Tax credits reward good business—innovation, hiring, sustainability, and benefits. Make them part of your annual strategy, not an afterthought.*

## KEY TAKEAWAY

The tax code is filled with incentives for entrepreneurs who create jobs, innovate, and improve their communities.

You're not just running a business—you're contributing to the economy. Claim the credits you've earned and reinvest those savings back into your growth.

Next up:
**Chapter 10 – Real Estate & Depreciation**
→ Learn how to turn real estate, equipment, and assets into powerful tax-saving tools through depreciation and smart structuring.

## *Chapter 10*

# Real Estate & Depreciation

*Turning Property and Equipment Into Powerful Tax Tools*

For many small business owners, real estate and equipment are the most significant investments they'll ever make.

Whether you own your building, lease office space, or buy equipment for your trade, the tax code offers major benefits for these assets—if you know how to use them.

This chapter explains how to legally reduce taxes by **depreciating** your business property, understanding **Section 179** and **bonus depreciation**, and strategically managing your **real estate holdings**.

## THE POWER OF DEPRECIATION

**Depreciation** is a tax deduction that allows you to recover the cost of business property over time as it "wears out" or becomes obsolete.

It's one of the most valuable—yet misunderstood—tools in small business taxation.

Simply put: depreciation lets you turn large purchases into annual deductions that reduce taxable income, even though you didn't spend that money this year.

**Example:**

You buy $30,000 of equipment.
Rather than deducting it all at once, you may depreciate it over 5 years → $6,000 per year deduction.
Or, if you qualify, deduct it all immediately under Section 179 (see below).

**Pro Tip:** *Depreciation is a non-cash expense—it lowers taxable income without affecting your bank balance.*

## WHAT QUALIFIES FOR DEPRECIATION

The IRS allows depreciation for property that:

1. You own (or lease with a capital lease),
2. Is used in your business, and
3. Has a determinable useful life of more than one year.

Common examples include:

1. Buildings and improvements
2. Office furniture and fixtures
3. Equipment and machinery
4. Computers and technology
5. Vehicles used for business
6. Tenant improvements

**Avoid This Mistake:** Personal-use property doesn't qualify. Only items used **more than 50% for business** are eligible for depreciation.

## METHODS OF DEPRECIATION

Most small businesses use the **Modified Accelerated Cost Recovery System (MACRS)**—the standard IRS method that allows faster deductions in the early years of ownership.

| Asset Type | Typical Recovery Period |
|---|---|
| Office furniture | 7 years |
| Computers & equipment | 5 years |
| Vehicles | 5 years |
| Residential rental property | 27.5 years |
| Commercial real estate | 39 years |

**Pro Tip:** *Ask your CPA to maintain a* **Fixed Asset Schedule***. This list tracks each asset's cost, purchase date, and remaining depreciation—essential for accurate tax and resale reporting.*

## SECTION 179: DEDUCT IT NOW

Section 179 allows you to **expense (deduct immediately)** the cost of qualifying equipment or software purchased for your business instead of spreading it over multiple years.

For 2025, the Section 179 limit is roughly **$1,220,000**, with a phase-out beginning at about **$3 million** in total purchases.

**Example:**

You buy new machinery for $25,000. Under Section 179, you can deduct the full $25,000 this year rather than over five years.

*Quick Checklist: Section 179 Eligibility*

- ☑ Must be tangible property (equipment, computers, vehicles, furniture)
- ☑ Must be used over 50% for business
- ☑ Must be purchased and placed in service before year-end
- ☑ Can't exceed taxable business income for the year

**Pro Tip:** *If your business has a strong year, Section 179 can offset profits quickly. In slower years, spread depreciation to future periods when income is higher.*

**Avoid This Mistake:** Expensing everything in one year without cash flow planning. A big deduction is great—unless it leaves no write-offs for next year.

## BONUS DEPRECIATION

**Bonus depreciation** allows you to deduct a percentage of an asset's cost in the first year—currently **60% in 2025**, gradually phasing down from 100% (pre-2023).

It can be combined with Section 179 to maximize upfront deductions.

| Year | Bonus Depreciation Rate |
|---|---|
| 2023 | 80% |
| 2024 | 60% |
| 2025 | 60% (expected) |
| 2026 | 40% |
| 2027 | 20% |

**Pro Tip:** *Unlike Section 179, bonus depreciation can* **create or increase a business loss**, *making it great for startups or expansion years.*

## REAL ESTATE: OWNING VS. LEASING

Should your business **own** its real estate—or **lease** it?

The right answer depends on your goals, growth plans, and tax strategy.

**Owning:**

- Builds equity and long-term wealth
- Offers depreciation and interest deductions
- Provides stability (no rent increases)
- Requires down payment and maintenance

**Leasing:**

- Conserves cash flow
- Provides flexibility to relocate or expand
- Deducts full rent payments
- No asset management headaches

**Example:**

If you buy a $500,000 building, you can depreciate the structure (not land) over 39 years → about $12,800 annual deduction.

Meanwhile, interest and property taxes are also deductible.

> **Pro Tip:** *Separate your* **operating business** *from your* **real estate ownership**—*hold property in an LLC and lease it to your company.*

This provides liability protection and allows you to shift income between entities strategically.

**Avoid This Mistake:** Failing to separate building cost from land. Land is not depreciable—only improvements and the structure are.

## COST SEGREGATION STUDIES

For property-heavy businesses (real estate investors, restaurants, manufacturers), a **cost segregation study** can accelerate depreciation.

This process identifies portions of a building (like electrical systems, flooring, or lighting) that qualify for shorter depreciation lives (5, 7, or 15 years).

**Example:**

A $1 million commercial building could yield $100,000+ in extra first-year deductions through cost segregation.

> **Pro Tip:** *This strategy works best for properties over $500,000 or when planning a sale in the next few years.*

## VEHICLE DEPRECIATION

Business vehicles may qualify for Section 179 or bonus depreciation.

Heavy SUVs, trucks, and vans with a **gross vehicle weight (GVW) over 6,000 lbs** are eligible for up to **100% first-year write-offs** (subject to limits).

*Quick Checklist: Vehicle Depreciation*

- ☑ Verify GVW rating > 6,000 lbs
- ☑ Use >50% for business purposes
- ☑ Title vehicle under business name
- ☑ Track mileage and expenses separately
- ☑ Claim either Section 179 or bonus—not both fully

**Pro Tip:** *Luxury vehicles have depreciation caps—heavy vehicles do not. Timing and classification are everything.*

## WHEN YOU SELL AN ASSET

When you sell depreciated property, the IRS may "recapture" some depreciation as **ordinary income**, rather than capital gain.

This is known as **Depreciation Recapture**.

**Example:**
You depreciate $20,000 on an asset purchased for $50,000 and later sell it for $45,000.

You'll recognize $15,000 as gain—but $20,000 of prior depreciation could be recaptured at ordinary rates.

**Pro Tip:** *When planning a sale, review your depreciation history. Properly timing or structuring the sale (like using a 1031 exchange) can defer taxes.*

## REAL ESTATE FOR RETIREMENT

Many entrepreneurs buy property not only for their business but also as part of their **retirement strategy**—creating income and appreciation for decades.

**Pro Tip:** *You can own real estate inside certain* **self-directed retirement plans** *(like a Solo 401(k) or SDIRA). This allows rental income and gains to grow tax-deferred—but requires careful compliance.*

**Avoid This Mistake:** Using personal funds or benefiting directly from property inside a retirement account—it triggers prohibited transaction penalties.

## KEY TAKEAWAY

Depreciation and real estate ownership are not just accounting concepts—they're wealth-building levers. Used wisely, they help you grow your assets, lower your taxes, and keep your money working for you long after the initial purchase.

*Quick Recap Checklist*

- ☑ Track and classify all business assets
- ☑ Use Section 179 for immediate deductions
- ☑ Leverage bonus depreciation strategically
- ☑ Separate operating and real estate entities
- ☑ Review depreciation schedules annually

**Pro Tip:** *Depreciation is how the tax code rewards long-term thinking. Every asset tells a story—make sure yours is written for maximum advantage.*

Next up:

**Chapter 11 – Business Sale & Exit Tax Strategies**

→ Learn how to sell your business or assets wisely, minimize capital gains, and exit with confidence and clarity.

*Chapter 11*

# Business Sale & Exit Tax Strategies

*How to Sell Your Business (or Assets) the Smart, Tax-Efficient Way*

Every business owner dreams of a successful exit—whether it's selling your company, retiring, or passing it on to the next generation.

But here's what many don't realize: how you structure that exit determines **how much of your hard-earned wealth you keep.**

Selling a business is both a financial and emotional event. The key is to plan early, understand your options, and structure the deal in a way that minimizes taxes and maximizes your legacy.

## WHY EXIT PLANNING MATTERS

Most business owners spend years building their company—but only hours planning their exit.

The result? They often pay **far more in taxes** than necessary and lose control of the timing and terms.

Exit planning isn't about quitting—it's about creating freedom and optionality.

When you're ready to sell (or step back), your business should be positioned to transfer smoothly and profitably.

> **Pro Tip:** *Start planning your exit* **2–5 years before** *you expect to sell. This window allows you to improve valuation, clean up records, and implement tax-saving structures.*

## STEP 1: KNOW WHAT YOU'RE SELLING

The IRS treats sales differently depending on whether you sell **assets** or **stock (ownership interests).**

| Type of Sale | You Sell | Typical Buyer Preference | Typical Seller Preference | Tax Treatment |
|---|---|---|---|---|
| **Asset Sale** | Individual assets of the business | ☑ Buyer | × Seller | Mostly ordinary income (depreciation recapture) |
| **Stock Sale (or Membership Interest)** | Ownership in the entity | × Buyer | ☑ Seller | Typically capital gains (lower rates) |

**Example:**
You own an S-Corp valued at $1 million.

- **Asset sale:** You might owe ordinary income tax on $200k of depreciation recapture.
- **Stock sale:** You might pay long-term capital gains on the entire $1 million at 15–20%.

> **Pro Tip:** *Whenever possible, negotiate a* **stock sale** *(or membership interest sale for LLCs). It's simpler and generally more tax-efficient for the seller.*

**Avoid This Mistake:** Letting the buyer's accountant drive the structure. Their goal is to maximize deductions—yours should be to minimize taxable income.

## STEP 2: UNDERSTAND CAPITAL GAINS

If you sell your business or property for more than your basis (the original investment plus improvements, minus depreciation), the difference is a **capital gain.**

| Type of Gain | Holding Period | Tax Rate |
|---|---|---|
| **Short-Term** | Held ≤ 1 year | Ordinary income rates (10–37%) |
| **Long-Term** | Held > 1 year | 0%, 15%, or 20% (plus 3.8% NIIT if applicable) |

**Pro Tip:** *Hold ownership for at least* **12 months** *before selling to qualify for long-term capital gains—this can cut your tax bill nearly in half.*

## STEP 3: ALLOCATE THE PURCHASE PRICE STRATEGICALLY

In an **asset sale**, the purchase price must be allocated among different categories—each with unique tax outcomes.

| Category | Buyer's Treatment | Seller's Treatment |
|---|---|---|
| Inventory | Deductible | Ordinary income |
| Equipment | Depreciable | Depreciation recapture (ordinary income) |
| Goodwill | Amortized over 15 years | Long-term capital gain |
| Real Estate | Depreciable | Part capital gain, part recapture |

**Pro Tip:** *Negotiate allocation carefully—it can mean tens of thousands in tax difference. Buyers want more value in depreciable assets; sellers want more in goodwill or stock.*

**Avoid This Mistake:** Accepting the buyer's allocation without review. Always involve your CPA before signing.

## STEP 4: CONSIDER INSTALLMENT SALES

If the buyer pays you over time (e.g., 3–5 years), you can use the **installment method** to spread your tax liability.

- You recognize gain proportionally as payments are received.
- Interest on deferred payments is taxable as ordinary income.

**Example:**
You sell your business for $500,000—$100,000 down and $400,000 over four years.

Instead of paying tax on $500,000 in one year, you spread it out, reducing your overall rate and easing cash flow.

**Pro Tip:** *Installment sales can be ideal for internal buyouts, family transfers, or when you trust the buyer's ongoing ability to pay.*

**Avoid This Mistake:** Failing to charge interest. The IRS requires a minimum interest rate (the "Applicable Federal Rate," or AFR) on installment notes.

## STEP 5: USE 1031 EXCHANGES (FOR REAL ESTATE)

If part of your business includes real estate, you can defer capital gains by using a **1031 Like-Kind Exchange**—reinvesting sale proceeds into another business or investment property.

*Quick Checklist: 1031 Requirements*

- ☑ Property must be held for business or investment (not personal use)
- ☑ Identify replacement property within 45 days
- ☑ Close on replacement property within 180 days
- ☑ Use a qualified intermediary to hold funds

**Pro Tip:** *A 1031 exchange doesn't eliminate tax—it* **defers** *it. When done repeatedly, it can grow your wealth tax-deferred for decades.*

**Avoid This Mistake:** Taking possession of funds, even briefly. That invalidates the exchange.

## STEP 6: QUALIFIED SMALL BUSINESS STOCK (QSBS)

If your company is a **C-Corporation** and meets certain criteria, selling stock may qualify for the **Section 1202 exclusion**, which can eliminate up to **$10 million** of capital gains.

Requirements include:

- Held stock for at least 5 years
- Corporation has ≤ $50 million in assets
- Active U.S. business (not passive investing or services)

> **Pro Tip:** *QSBS can be a game-changer for high-growth companies or startups—consult a tax attorney early to qualify.*

## STEP 7: GIFTING, LEGACY, AND SUCCESSION PLANNING

If your goal isn't to sell but to **pass your business to family**, proper planning can minimize estate and gift taxes.

Options include:

- **Gradual ownership transfer** through annual gifting (up to $18,000 per person per year, 2025 limit).
- **Family Limited Partnerships (FLPs)** for controlled transfers.
- **Buy-sell agreements** for smooth succession among partners.

> **Pro Tip:** *Work with both a* **CPA and estate attorney** *to coordinate your business, personal assets, and family goals.*

**Avoid This Mistake:** Waiting until illness or retirement to plan your exit. Succession is a process, not an event.

## STEP 8: CLEAN UP BEFORE THE SALE

Preparing your business for sale is like staging a house—presentation matters.

Buyers pay more for businesses with clean books, solid systems, and predictable cash flow.

*Quick Checklist: Pre-Sale Readiness*

- ☑ Update financial statements and reconcile all accounts
- ☑ Pay off unnecessary debts or simplify balance sheet
- ☑ Document contracts, leases, and customer agreements
- ☑ Organize corporate records and entity filings
- ☑ Review tax returns for consistency and clarity

**Pro Tip:** *A "tax-clean" business commands a higher price. Buyers trust organized books—and the IRS stays away from red flags.*

## STEP 9: INVOLVE YOUR ADVISORY TEAM EARLY

You'll need three key professionals:

1. **CPA or Tax Strategist** – to model scenarios and minimize taxes
2. **Business Broker or Advisor** – to find and qualify buyers
3. **Attorney** – to draft agreements and protect your interests

**Pro Tip:** *Your CPA should run multiple projections—stock vs. asset sale, lump sum vs. installment, cash vs. seller financing—to help you choose the optimal structure.*

## STEP 10: PLAN FOR LIFE AFTER THE SALE

After the sale closes, you'll likely face a large liquidity event.

Now the focus shifts to **protecting and investing** your proceeds wisely.

*Quick Checklist: Post-Sale Planning*

- ☑ Set aside tax reserves for any remaining liabilities
- ☑ Meet with a financial planner to design a diversified portfolio
- ☑ Review insurance, estate plans, and charitable goals
- ☑ Consider donor-advised funds for tax-efficient giving

**Pro Tip:** *A well-planned sale not only creates financial freedom—it preserves your legacy and values beyond the business itself.*

## KEY TAKEAWAY

Selling your business is one of the biggest financial decisions of your life.

With thoughtful structure, professional guidance, and tax planning, you can exit confidently—keeping more of what you built and securing your financial future.

*Quick Recap Checklist*

- ☑ Plan your exit 2–5 years ahead
- ☑ Favor stock sales over asset sales when possible
- ☑ Consider installment or 1031 options
- ☑ Use QSBS if applicable
- ☑ Coordinate with CPA, attorney, and financial planner

**Pro Tip:** *The ultimate goal of tax strategy isn't just saving money—it's achieving peace, purpose, and freedom for your next chapter.*

**Chapter 12 – Working With a CPA (and What to Expect)**
→ How to build a strong partnership with your CPA, what to bring to meetings, and how to get the most value from professional tax advice.

# Chapter 12

# Working With a CPA (and What to Expect)

*How to Build a Trusted Partnership That Saves You Time, Taxes, and Stress*

Behind every thriving small business is a great financial team—at the center of that team is your **CPA**.

Your Certified Public Accountant is more than a tax preparer; they're a strategic partner who helps you grow, protect, and sustain your business financially.

The right CPA doesn't just help you file your return—they help you plan your future.

## WHY EVERY SMALL BUSINESS NEEDS A CPA

Many entrepreneurs start out doing their own bookkeeping or using tax software. That's fine at first, but as your business grows, complexity grows too.

You need someone who understands how your *numbers tell a story.*

A great CPA can help you:

- Structure your business for tax efficiency
- Identify deductions and credits you're missing
- Plan quarterly estimates and cash flow
- Prepare for expansion, hiring, or exit strategies
- Represent you before the IRS if needed

**Pro Tip:** *Think of your CPA as part of your leadership team—not just a service provider. Bring them into your planning conversations early.*

## WHAT A CPA ACTUALLY DOES

CPAs provide a wide range of services that go far beyond tax filing. Here's a breakdown:

| Service Type | What It Includes | Benefit to You |
|---|---|---|
| **Tax Preparation** | Filing federal, state, and local returns | Accuracy & compliance |
| **Tax Planning** | Strategies to minimize taxes throughout the year | Saves money long-term |
| **Bookkeeping & Accounting** | Managing transactions, reconciling accounts | Keeps financials organized |
| **Financial Statements** | Profit & Loss, Balance Sheet, Cash Flow | Lender & investor confidence |
| **Payroll Services** | Tax filings, W-2s, 1099s, withholdings | Legal compliance |
| **Advisory & Strategy** | Forecasting, business growth, exit planning | Future-focused decision making |

**Pro Tip:** *Tax prep looks backward—advisory looks forward. Choose a CPA who does both.*

## CHOOSING THE RIGHT CPA

**Not all accountants are the same**. Some focus on individuals, others on corporations or specific industries.

For small business owners, look for a CPA who specializes in **entrepreneurship and small business taxation.**

*Quick Checklist: How to Choose Your CPA*

- ☑ Licensed and in good standing (check your state board)
- ☑ Experience with your entity type (LLC, S-Corp, etc.)
- ☑ Familiar with your industry or niche
- ☑ Offers year-round access, not just tax season
- ☑ Provides proactive advice and planning
- ☑ Communicates clearly and avoids jargon

**Pro Tip:** *Ask potential CPAs, "How will you help me plan ahead, not just file last year's numbers?" Their answer tells you everything.*

## WHEN TO INVOLVE YOUR CPA

Most small business owners make the mistake of contacting their accountant only once a year—around tax time.

By then, most opportunities for tax savings are gone.

Here's the better rhythm:

| Frequency | Meeting Type | Focus |
|---|---|---|
| **Monthly or Quarterly** | Bookkeeping & financial review | Cash flow, estimated taxes |
| **Mid-Year (June–July)** | Tax projection & planning | Adjust payments, review deductions |
| **Year-End (Nov–Dec)** | Tax strategy & prep for filing | Time major purchases, contributions |
| **As Needed** | Major decisions | Entity change, hiring, or expansion |

**Pro Tip:** *Your CPA can't change what's already happened—but they can optimize what's ahead. Meet before year-end, not after.*

**Avoid This Mistake:** Treating your CPA like a last-minute problem solver. Their best work happens when they're part of your ongoing decision-making.

## WHAT TO BRING TO CPA MEETINGS

The more prepared you are, the more valuable your meetings become.

*Quick Checklist: CPA Meeting Essentials*

- ☑ Updated bookkeeping or profit & loss reports
- ☑ Year-to-date bank statements
- ☑ Payroll and 1099 summaries
- ☑ Receipts for large purchases or new assets
- ☑ Estimated tax payments made
- ☑ Questions about upcoming plans (hiring, real estate, etc.)

**Pro Tip:** *Keep a running "tax notes" file throughout the year—questions, purchases, and milestones. Bring it to every CPA meeting.*

## HOW TO COMMUNICATE EFFECTIVELY

Good communication turns your CPA into a trusted advisor instead of a transactional vendor.

Do:

- Ask "what if" questions before making major moves.
- Be honest about cash flow, debt, and challenges.
- Respond quickly to document requests.
- Schedule meetings instead of relying solely on email.

Don't:

- Wait until April to drop off a shoebox of receipts.
- Assume your CPA automatically knows your plans.
- Ignore IRS or state correspondence—bring it to them immediately.

**Pro Tip:** *Strong relationships produce better results. The more your CPA understands your business, the more strategic and creative they can be on your behalf.*

## WORKING WITH BOOKKEEPERS AND ACCOUNTANTS

Your CPA may coordinate with bookkeepers, payroll providers, or in-house staff. Each plays a role:

| Role | Focus | Frequency |
|---|---|---|
| **Bookkeeper** | Day-to-day transactions, categorizing, reconciling | Weekly or monthly |
| **Accountant** | Prepares reports, monitors accounts, supports CPA | Monthly or quarterly |
| **CPA** | Reviews, advises, files, and plans | Quarterly or annually |

**Pro Tip:** *Think of it like building a financial pyramid—bookkeeping is the foundation, accounting is the structure, and your CPA provides the view from the top.*

## HOW CPAS SAVE YOU MONEY

A skilled CPA can:

- Optimize your entity structure (LLC vs. S-Corp)
- Time purchases for maximum deductions
- Identify missed credits and write-offs
- Advise on payroll and owner compensation
- Strategize for retirement and exit planning

**Example:**
A client earning $100,000 as an LLC elects S-Corp status on their CPA's advice, saving $7,000 in self-employment taxes annually.

That's real money—created by one informed decision.

**Pro Tip:** *Good tax planning often pays for itself many times over. Think of your CPA's fee as an investment, not an expense.*

## QUESTIONS TO ASK YOUR CPA

*Quick Checklist: CPA Conversation Starters*

1. What are the biggest tax-saving opportunities for my type of business?
2. Should I consider changing my business structure this year?
3. What are the top deductions or credits people in my industry miss?
4. How should I handle paying myself (draw, salary, or distribution)?
5. Are there any IRS or state changes I should prepare for next year?
6. How can I make my recordkeeping easier for both of us?
7. What can I do before year-end to reduce next year's tax bill?

**Pro Tip:** *Come prepared with your own agenda—it turns every CPA meeting into a strategy session, not just a data dump.*

## HOW TO GET THE MOST VALUE FROM YOUR CPA

The best relationships are partnerships. To maximize the value:

- Communicate regularly and proactively.
- Ask them to review your numbers mid-year.
- Discuss both business and personal financial goals.
- Request plain-English explanations—you deserve to understand your money.
- Build long-term trust through consistency and openness.

**Pro Tip:** *Your CPA can't read your mind, but they can transform your business—if you invite them into your bigger vision.*

## KEY TAKEAWAY

A great CPA is not a cost—they're a catalyst.

They help you stay compliant, plan strategically, and grow sustainably.

*Quick Recap Checklist*

- ☑ Hire a CPA experienced with small businesses
- ☑ Meet quarterly (not just annually)
- ☑ Bring organized records and clear goals
- ☑ Treat them as a partner, not a processor
- ☑ Ask smart, forward-looking questions

**Pro Tip:** *The best financial partnerships are built on trust, transparency, and teamwork. Choose wisely—and invest in that relationship like it's part of your business itself.*

Next up:

**Chapter 13 – Year-End Checklist & Tax Calendar**

→ Your month-by-month guide to staying ahead of deadlines, organizing documents, and making year-end tax season smooth and stress-free.

*Chapter 13*

# Year-End Checklist & Tax Calendar

*Stay Organized, Avoid Surprises, and Finish Every Year Strong*

Tax season should never feel like a race against the clock.

With a structured year-end process and clear deadlines, you can transform what's usually a scramble into a smooth, predictable rhythm.

This chapter gives you a **month-by-month calendar**, a **master checklist**, and a few simple systems to keep your business tax-ready all year long.

## WHY YEAR-END PLANNING MATTERS

Most small business owners wait until January to think about taxes—when it's too late to make strategic moves.

Real savings happen **before December 31**.

Year-end planning helps you:

- Maximize deductions before the deadline
- Avoid missed filings or penalties
- Forecast cash flow and profit accurately
- Reduce stress and CPA costs at filing time

**Pro Tip:** *Think of December 31 as your "scoreboard reset." The game isn't over, but next year's success starts now.*

## MONTHLY TAX & RECORDKEEPING CALENDAR

Use this as your recurring guide for the year ahead.

| Month | Key Actions | Notes |
|---|---|---|
| **January** | Send W-2s & 1099-NECs (by Jan 31); Pay Q4 estimates (due Jan 15); Close prior year books | Start fresh budget for the new year |
| **February** | Review bank and credit card statements; gather year-end documents | Give CPA organized files early |
| **March** | File partnership & S-Corp returns (Form 1065/1120-S due Mar 15); Finalize personal extensions if needed | Avoid last-minute rush |
| **April** | File individual returns & C-Corp returns (Apr 15); Pay Q1 estimated tax | Verify EFTPS payment records |
| **May – June** | Mid-year review of profit & loss; adjust quarterly payments | Schedule a tax projection meeting with CPA |
| **July** | Audit your books; clean up categories & receipts | Prepare for Q3 planning |
| **September** | Pay Q3 estimated tax (Sept 15); evaluate retirement contributions | Fine-tune deductions |
| **October** | File extended returns (if applies, Oct 15); start year-end planning | Time major purchases |
| **November** | Meet with CPA for final tax strategy session | Lock in Section 179 or bonus depreciation moves |
| **December** | Finalize payroll & bonus payouts; review charitable giving; record mileage and inventory | Close books by Dec 31 |

**Pro Tip:** *Print this table and post it near your desk or inside your planner. Treat each quarter like a mini tax season—lighter, faster, and less stressful.*

## THE YEAR-END FINANCIAL CHECKLIST

*Quick Checklist: Close Your Books Like a Pro*

- ☑ Reconcile all bank and credit accounts
- ☑ Categorize every expense through Dec 31
- ☑ Record depreciation and loan interest
- ☑ Verify accounts receivable and payable
- ☑ Count and value inventory
- ☑ Confirm owner draws or salary amounts
- ☑ Update mileage logs and home-office records
- ☑ Gather W-9s from all contractors
- ☑ Prepare 1099s and W-2s for January
- ☑ Back up all digital records and accounting files

**Pro Tip:** *The cleaner your books, the cheaper (and faster) your CPA's work will be.*

## PRE-TAX SEASON ORGANIZATION

Organize documents into four folders—digital or physical:

1. **Income** – Invoices, sales reports, 1099s received
2. **Expenses** – Receipts, statements, vendor records
3. **Assets & Depreciation** – Equipment purchases, leases, real estate files
4. **Tax Forms & Correspondence** – Prior returns, IRS letters, quarterly payment proof

**Pro Tip:** *Label folders by year and store copies in cloud storage (e.g., Google Drive, Dropbox). Future-you will thank you.*

## YEAR-END TAX-SAVING MOVES

As December approaches, there are still ways to lower your tax bill legally and effectively.

### Top Moves Before December 31

- **Fund retirement plans** (SEP, Solo 401(k), SIMPLE)
- **Buy and place equipment in service** for Section 179 deduction
- **Prepay expenses** (e.g., rent, supplies, marketing campaigns)
- **Review outstanding invoices** – collect now or delay income if cash-basis
- **Make charitable contributions** by year-end
- **Evaluate bonus depreciation** for vehicles or equipment

**Pro Tip:** *The best time to save on taxes is before December 31. After that, you're just reporting history.*

## PAYROLL & CONTRACTOR DEADLINES

| Task | Due Date | Form |
|---|---|---|
| Issue W-2s to employees | Jan 31 | W-2 |
| File Form W-3 (Summary) | Jan 31 | W-3 |
| Issue 1099-NECs to contractors | Jan 31 | 1099-NEC |
| File Form 940 (FUTA Annual) | Jan 31 | 940 |
| File Form 941 (Q4 Payroll Tax Return) | Jan 31 | 941 |

**Avoid This Mistake:** Waiting until January to request W-9s from contractors. Collect them as soon as you pay $600 or more in a calendar year.

## PREPARING FOR NEXT YEAR

*Quick Checklist: Start Strong*

- ☑ Set aside monthly tax savings (20–30% of profit)
- ☑ Review your entity status with your CPA
- ☑ Update your budget and profit targets
- ☑ Schedule quarterly check-ins for the year
- ☑ Reset financial goals and personal compensation plan

**Pro Tip:** *Begin each January with clarity, not catch-up. A simple plan and steady rhythm beat a last-minute rush every time.*

## AUTOMATE REMINDERS AND ROUTINES

Set recurring calendar alerts for:

- Quarterly tax payments
- Payroll submission deadlines
- Monthly reconciliation tasks
- CPA meeting dates
- Year-end prep checklist review

**Pro Tip:** *Use Google Calendar or Asana to create recurring reminders for tax deadlines. You'll never miss a due date again.*

## KEY TAKEAWAY

Great tax planning is just great organization in disguise.

When you make tax tasks part of your monthly routine, you turn a once-a-year headache into a year-round advantage.

*Quick Recap Checklist*

- ☑ Follow the monthly calendar above
- ☑ Complete the year-end checklist by Dec 31
- ☑ Meet with your CPA before year-end
- ☑ File all forms by January deadlines
- ☑ Start the new year with clean books and a clear plan

**Pro Tip:** *Organization isn't just a trait—it's a profit strategy. Every minute you spend staying ahead of the IRS gives you more time to focus on what you do best: building your business.*

Next up:

**Chapter 14 – Avoiding the IRS Audit Trap**

→ Learn what triggers audits, how to stay compliant, and what to do if the IRS comes knocking.

*Chapter 14*

# Avoiding the IRS Audit Trap

*How to Stay Compliant, Reduce Red Flags, and Sleep Well at Night*

Few words make business owners more nervous than "IRS audit."

But here's the truth: if your books are clean, your deductions are legitimate, and your documentation is strong, you have nothing to fear.

Audits aren't random—they're usually triggered by patterns, inconsistencies, or lack of documentation.

This chapter helps you understand **what causes audits**, **how to avoid red flags**, and **what to do if you're ever selected.**

## WHY THE IRS AUDITS BUSINESSES

The IRS uses data analytics and algorithms (called the *Discriminant Inventory Function System*, or DIF) to flag returns that look unusual compared to similar businesses.

They're looking for:

- Missing or mismatched income
- Excessive deductions relative to income
- Unusual business losses or large write-offs
- Math errors or inconsistent records

**Pro Tip:** *Audits are about patterns, not punishment. A well-documented business that plays by the rules will always stand strong under review.*

## COMMON SMALL BUSINESS AUDIT TRIGGERS

Here are the most frequent red flags the IRS looks for in small business returns:

| Red Flag | Why It Raises Suspicion | How to Avoid It |
|---|---|---|
| **High deductions vs. income** | IRS compares ratios by industry averages | Keep receipts and justify deductions |
| **Excessive meal or travel claims** | Commonly overstated by small businesses | Keep logs and business purpose for every trip |
| **Large vehicle deductions** | Vehicles often used personally | Maintain mileage logs & proof of business use |
| **Unreported income** | IRS receives 1099s & W-2s electronically | Match all reported income—every time |
| **Home office deduction abuse** | Misunderstood rules | Use only exclusive, regular-use spaces |
| **Continuous losses (Schedule C)** | May signal hobby, not business | Show profit motive & business activity |
| **Rounding or estimates** | Suggests guesswork, not records | Use exact amounts from bookkeeping software |

**Avoid This Mistake:** Guessing numbers or "ballparking" expenses. The IRS assumes imprecision equals inaccuracy. Always back up with documentation.

## THE POWER OF DOCUMENTATION

When it comes to audits, **proof beats panic** every time.

*Quick Checklist: What to Keep*

- Receipts and invoices (digital or paper)
- Bank and credit card statements
- Mileage logs
- Contracts and agreements
- Proof of payment (cancelled checks, transaction records)
- Meeting notes or calendars showing business purpose

**Pro Tip:** *Digitize everything. Cloud-based document storage (Google Drive, OneDrive, Dropbox) makes retrieval simple and secure.*

## UNDERSTANDING AUDIT TYPES

Not all audits are equal. Some are quick letters; others are in-depth reviews.

| Type | Description | Typical Response Time |
|---|---|---|
| **Correspondence Audit** | Done entirely by mail—usually one or two issues | 30–60 days |
| **Office Audit** | You meet with an IRS agent locally | 60–90 days |
| **Field Audit** | IRS visits your business | 90+ days (in-depth review) |

**Pro Tip:** *If you receive a notice, stay calm. Read it carefully—it tells you exactly what the IRS wants. Never ignore or delay your response.*

## HOW TO HANDLE AN IRS NOTICE

If you receive a letter from the IRS, it doesn't automatically mean you're in trouble.

Most notices are corrections, missing forms, or requests for clarification.

*Quick Checklist: Responding to IRS Notices*

1. **Read the entire notice** – note any deadlines.
2. **Compare it to your tax return** – look for mismatched figures.
3. **Gather documentation** to support your position.
4. **Contact your CPA immediately** – don't go it alone.
5. **Respond before the due date** (usually 30 days).
6. **Keep copies** of all correspondence sent and received.

**Pro Tip:** *If you respond promptly and professionally, most small discrepancies are resolved quickly without penalties.*

**Avoid This Mistake:** Ignoring IRS mail or letting fear delay action. Silence can turn a small issue into a large one.

## HOW TO AUDIT-PROOF YOUR BUSINESS

The best audit defense is a solid offense: good systems, accurate books, and consistent compliance.

*Quick Checklist: Audit-Proof Habits*

- ☑ Reconcile your books monthly
- ☑ Keep business and personal accounts separate
- ☑ Track vehicle mileage in real time
- ☑ Label receipts with client names or project codes
- ☑ Review deductions quarterly with your CPA
- ☑ File on time and pay estimated taxes

**Pro Tip:** *Keep your tax returns and supporting records for* **at least seven years.** *That's the typical statute of limitations for audit review in complex cases.*

## THE ROLE OF YOUR CPA DURING AN AUDIT

Your CPA can act as your representative before the IRS—communicating, negotiating, and resolving the issue on your behalf.

They can:

- Review notices and draft responses
- Represent you in meetings or calls
- Verify IRS calculations and challenge errors
- Negotiate payment or penalty relief if needed

> **Pro Tip:** *If you're ever audited,* **never go alone.** *Always have a CPA or Enrolled Agent present. They understand IRS language and procedures far better than most taxpayers.*

## WHAT HAPPENS IF YOU OWE MORE

If an audit finds you owe additional taxes, you still have options:

1. **Pay immediately** (if minor).
2. **Request a payment plan (installment agreement).**
3. **Appeal the findings** within 30 days of the final report.

> **Pro Tip:** *The IRS often waives penalties for first-time offenders with a good compliance history. Ask your CPA about the* **First-Time Abatement** *program.*

## HOW TO LOWER YOUR AUDIT RISK

Some things are within your control. Consistency, documentation, and professional filing are your best shields.

| Strategy | Why It Works |
|---|---|
| File electronically | Reduces math errors and lost mail |
| Use CPA-prepared returns | Professional accuracy and representation |
| Keep consistent year-to-year deductions | Sudden changes draw attention |
| Avoid large "miscellaneous" categories | Detail your expenses clearly |
| Respond promptly to all IRS correspondence | Builds credibility and trust |

**Pro Tip:** *Honesty + organization = confidence. The IRS audits fewer than 1% of small businesses each year. Focus your energy on accuracy, not anxiety.*

## KEY TAKEAWAY

Audits aren't the enemy—disorganization is.

By maintaining clear records, reporting honestly, and partnering with a qualified CPA, you can protect your business, your time, and your peace of mind.

*Quick Recap Checklist*

- ☑ Keep all receipts, records, and mileage logs
- ☑ File accurately and on time
- ☑ Review red flags with your CPA annually
- ☑ Respond promptly to any IRS correspondence
- ☑ Stay calm and professional if selected for review

**Pro Tip:** *The goal isn't to "avoid" the IRS—it's to be ready if they ever call. Preparation turns fear into confidence.*

Next up:
**Chapter 15 – The Entrepreneur's Financial Mindset**
→ A closing chapter that ties it all together—mindset, stewardship, and the habits that lead to long-term financial freedom as a small business owner.

*Chapter 15*

# The Entrepreneur's Financial Mindset

*The Habits, Stewardship, and Perspective That Build Long-Term Freedom*

At its core, business finance is not just about numbers—it's about mindset.

Your beliefs about money, stewardship, and discipline shape the way you lead, spend, save, and give.

Taxes are part of that story, but they're not the whole story.

The most successful entrepreneurs don't just *avoid* tax problems—they cultivate a **financial mindset** that helps them build sustainable wealth and purpose.

## 1. THINK LIKE A STEWARD, NOT JUST AN EARNER

Every dollar that flows through your hands is a tool—something to manage, multiply, and direct toward impact.

When you adopt a steward's mindset, taxes become part of the responsibility, not a burden.

> **Pro Tip:** *Approach your business as if you're managing something entrusted to you—not something owned by you. That shift changes how you handle money, time, and opportunity.*

**Avoid This Mistake:** Thinking of taxes as punishment. In truth, they're a sign of profit—and a reminder that your work is producing value.

## 2. KNOW YOUR NUMBERS

You can't lead what you don't measure.

Many business owners delegate their financials and never look at them—until something goes wrong.

That's a dangerous habit. Confidence in business grows from clarity with numbers.

*Quick Checklist: Financial Awareness Habits*

- ☑ Review your profit & loss monthly
- ☑ Track cash flow weekly
- ☑ Compare income trends year over year
- ☑ Revisit pricing and profitability quarterly
- ☑ Set annual revenue and savings targets

**Pro Tip:** *The more familiar you are with your numbers, the more peaceful tax season becomes. Knowledge replaces anxiety.*

## 3. KEEP A LONG-TERM PERSPECTIVE

Taxes feel heavy when you only see the short term.

But when you zoom out—thinking in 3-, 5-, or 10-year horizons—you begin to see the compounding effect of good decisions.

**Example:**
A business that saves just $500 a month in taxes and reinvests it for 10 years at 8% earns over **$90,000**.
Small, consistent actions lead to massive outcomes.

**Pro Tip:** *Play the long game. Use your business to create assets—systems, property, and savings—that work for you long after you stop working.*

## 4. SEPARATE PERSONAL AND BUSINESS IDENTITY

It's easy to blur the lines between "you" and "your business." But for clarity, accountability, and peace of mind, they must be distinct.

Keep separate accounts, budgets, and goals.

Your business is a vehicle that serves your personal mission—but it isn't your entire identity.

**Pro Tip:** *Ask yourself quarterly: Is my business serving my life, or is my life serving my business? Adjust accordingly.*

## 5. PRACTICE FINANCIAL DISCIPLINE

Discipline is the bridge between knowledge and freedom.

Every financially strong entrepreneur follows simple, repeatable habits—even when it's inconvenient.

*Quick Checklist: Financial Discipline Habits*

- ☑ Save for taxes monthly
- ☑ Set a percentage for profit, not leftovers
- ☑ Pay yourself regularly and responsibly
- ☑ Reinvest strategically, not impulsively
- ☑ Give generously and consistently

**Pro Tip:** *Systems beat willpower. Automate everything possible—savings transfers, payroll, retirement contributions—so discipline happens automatically.*

## 6. BUILD A TEAM OF ADVISORS

No one builds wealth alone.

Your CPA, bookkeeper, financial advisor, attorney, and insurance agent each bring a different strength to your financial life.

Your job is to lead the team—to ask questions, stay informed, and make wise decisions with their guidance.

> **Pro Tip:** *Meet with your advisory team at least once per year. Align your business goals, taxes, and investments so they all point in the same direction.*

**Avoid This Mistake:** Relying on one professional to do everything. Collaboration protects you from blind spots.

## 7. INTEGRATE PURPOSE WITH PROFIT

Money is a tool, not a goal.

When you align your profits with purpose—helping others, creating jobs, supporting causes—you build something much deeper than a balance sheet.

> **Pro Tip:** *Generosity is good business. Companies that give intentionally often experience stronger culture, community reputation, and internal satisfaction.*

## 8. KEEP LEARNING

The tax code changes. Markets shift. Technology evolves.

What doesn't change is the need for continual learning.

Invest in books, podcasts, courses, and professional development that sharpen your financial intelligence.

*Quick Checklist: Growth Plan*

- ☑ Read one finance or leadership book per quarter
- ☑ Take an annual business workshop or tax course
- ☑ Attend your CPA's year-end tax briefing
- ☑ Join a mastermind or business peer group

**Pro Tip:** *You don't rise to the level of your income—you rise to the level of your understanding.*

## 9. LIVE BELOW YOUR MEANS, DREAM ABOVE THEM

The real reward of owning a business isn't the car or the office—it's **freedom.**

Freedom to choose how you spend your time, invest your energy, and design your future.

Keep your lifestyle one step behind your income and your vision one step ahead of it.

That's how you stay motivated without becoming burdened.

**Pro Tip:** *When profits grow, don't inflate expenses—expand vision.*

## 10. REMEMBER WHY YOU STARTED

Behind every entrepreneur's story is a "why."

Maybe it was family, freedom, purpose, or calling. Whatever yours is, keep it close.

It's the compass that keeps you steady through every tax season, growth year, or lean month.

**Pro Tip:** *Revisit your vision annually. Your numbers serve your purpose, not the other way around.*

## KEY TAKEAWAY

Financial success starts with mindset.

When you lead your business with clarity, integrity, and intention, taxes become a manageable part of a much bigger picture: building something meaningful, lasting, and free.

*Quick Recap Checklist*

- ☑ Think long-term and act consistently
- ☑ Separate business from personal finances
- ☑ Stay disciplined and informed
- ☑ Build a trusted advisory team
- ☑ Align money with mission

**Pro Tip:** *Freedom isn't the absence of taxes—it's the mastery of them. When you understand the rules, use them wisely, and stay grateful for the opportunities you've built, you'll always be ahead.*

# Closing Words from Brandon K. Moore

Building a business is one of the most challenging and rewarding journeys you can take. I hope this guide has given you both practical tools and renewed confidence to handle your taxes—and your finances—with wisdom and peace.

Remember: stewardship, strategy, and simplicity go hand in hand.

Keep good records, plan ahead, and surround yourself with great people.

And above all, stay faithful in the little things—because consistency compounds.

Here's to your success,

**— Brandon K. Moore, CPA**

brandon@brandonkmoore.com

www.brandonkmoore.com

Made in the USA
Monee, IL
05 November 2026

67380147R00055